The SPD and European Integration

WILLIAM E. PATERSON

SAXON HOUSE | LEXINGTON BOOKS

Published by
SAXON HOUSE, D.C. Heath Ltd.
Westmead, Farnborough, Hants, England

Jointly with
LEXINGTON BOOKS, D.C. Heath & Co.
Lexington Mass. U.S.A.

ISBN 0 347 01040 7
Library of Congress Catalog Card Number 73-21193
Printed in Great Britain by Robert MacLehose & Co. Ltd
The University Press, Glasgow

Contents

5 EEC AND EURATOM — THE SPD CHANGES COURSE

6 THE SPD AND EUROPEAN INTEGRATION 1958—73

Preface

This book has its origins in a doctoral thesis for the London School of Economics. In transforming the thesis into a book I received many helpful suggestions from Ieuan John, Roger Morgan and Philip Windsor. I should also like to record my indebtedness to Kurt Schmitz, who has helped the completion of this study in innumerable ways, and to two librarians, the late Paul Mayer, the last librarian of the old SPD Executive Archive, and Frl. Hanna Jaede of the Deutsche Gesellschaft für Auswärtige Politik. Finally, my thanks are due to my wife, who helped greatly in the editing of the manuscript, and to Mrs Janet White, who did the typing.

Introduction

'There is nothing the Socialists nationalise
as quickly as socialism.'

Ignazio Silone
following *Borkenau.*

A study of the SPD and European integration in the early years of the
Federal Republic is interesting not only because of the questions raised
about the process of European integration, but also for the light it throws
on the evolution of West German domestic politics and the nature of
'opposition'.

The standard study on political parties and European integration, Ernst
Haas's *The Uniting of Europe*, delineates the reactions of the parties of
the Six to the successive attempts at constructing European institutions,
but fails to pay adequate attention to the domestic political arenas of
which these parties form a part.[1] In Haas's study, parties are analysed
almost exclusively in terms of a process of European integration. This
failure to analyse the domestic political dimension of the SPD's European
policy is the more unfortunate since it is part of a general neglect of the
interplay between domestic and external policy in studies on West Germany. However, omission of the domestic dimension in international relations is not peculiar to studies of West Germany. It is only a special case in
a general neglect which is only now beginning to be made good. Nevertheless, in the case of West Germany it is particularly damaging not to
consider the domestic dimension, since West German political parties have
functioned in a state created by foreign policy; a state which, even after
the formal occupation ceased in 1955, continued to act as a base for a
large number of foreign troops. Indeed, West Germany has served as the
primary model of the 'penetrated political system', a system in which the
major political decisions affecting the future of that society are taken
primarily by the leaders of other states.[2] In such a situation all the political parties have of necessity concentrated on the interconnections between domestic and foreign policy. In the case of the SPD I hope to show
that domestic factors within the West German political system were more
important in shaping the attitudes of the party to West European institutions than the form which the institutions took. To do this I shall examine
not only inter-party, but also intra-party, factors. These intra-party dis-

putes are important not only in deciding the formulation of a party's position, but also in indirectly reflecting larger issues affecting the whole political system.

The attempt by Haas to isolate and analyse an integration process, while ignoring the domestic political dimension, leads him to treat the SPD's opposition to the development of European institutions as purely obstructionist.[3] Apart from denying the right of an opposition to oppose, this approach seems to me implicitly to reflect a bias in favour of the integration phenomenon in Western Europe. An examination of the SPD's policy towards European integration in terms of what it was intended to achieve politically, and how effective it was in this sphere, seems more apposite than an analysis concerned exclusively with the degree to which this policy illustrates a process of European integration.

In addition, the study of the SPD in this period in relation to European integration provides a near-classical case study in opposition. Otto Kirchheimer, in his article 'The waning of the opposition in parliamentary regimes', isolated three basic models.[4] These are the classic English model of the loyal opposition; the opposition of principle, as with the position of the Nazi party in the Weimar period; and cartel arrangements operating within the framework of parliamentary institutions, as demonstrated by the coalition in post-war Austria. During the period covered by this study, the SPD policy on European integration appeared to approximate successively to these three models.

Kurt Schumacher, the first post-war leader, consciously attempted to establish an opposition on the classic English pattern, despite his rhetorical attachment to a 'policy of intransigence'. After his death in 1952 his conception of opposition was at first followed. However, the division of Germany rendered the ideal of 'loyal opposition' very difficult to achieve, since any opposition, especially in foreign affairs, could be interpreted as aiding the rival Pankow regime. The choice, therefore, seemed to lie more between 'opposition of principle' and coalition explicit or implicit. The SPD's opposition to the signature of the Western European Union Treaty, which reached its height in the 'Paulskirche movement', ('Paulskirche Bewegung'), resembled in its utilisation of extra-parliamentary means (a step never countenanced by Schumacher) 'opposition of principle'. For a complex of reasons, this was never a viable alternative, and was never wholeheartedly embraced by the SPD. Conversion to what was in effect the Christian-Democratic policy on European integration, and a more co-operative policy on defence, was coterminous with the collapse of the 'Paulskirche movement' shortly after its foundation in 1955. In the following years the SPD's policy on European affairs became for a time virtually indistinguishable from that of the CDU/CSU. In effect, despite residual opposition on foreign policy and atomic weapons up to the 1959 Deutschland plan, Kirchheimer's third model of no substantive opposition to government measures was adopted. In this model, the opposition hopes to shape governmental measures by accepting them in principle and confining 'opposition' to the tidying up of governmental measures in committees.

1 Historical Background

I intend to provide only a short background to the SPD's traditional attitude towards European integration, as pre-war attitudes are only tangentially relevant to this study, formulated as they were in the context of an undivided Germany.

The German Social Democratic Party traditionally conformed to the West European socialist tradition of according primacy to domestic, rather than foreign, policy. When it did express opinions on foreign policy issues, they were very similar to the principles stressed by Richard Rose in his 1960 Oxford D.Phil. thesis on 'The relation of socialist principles to British Labour foreign policy, 1945–51'.[5] These principles involved a belief in international co-operation, class consciousness in foreign affairs, supranationalism and anti-militarism. The belief in international co-operation and anti-militarism was always tempered by the Lasallean tradition of 'etatism', which was a crucial factor on vital occasions like the SPD vote on war credits in August 1914. The principle of class-consciousness in foreign affairs, strong in the British left, was weakened by a traditional Russophobia that can be traced as far back as Marx.

In accord with their general principles on foreign affairs, the idea of European unity was always popular with some individual SPD politicians. Otto Hue, the miners' leader, advanced as early as in 1912 the idea of concerted policy for the exploitation of European iron resources by means of a trade policy linking the East – which lacked iron resources – to Germany, and the formation of a Franco–German iron and steel community. This was envisaged as a step on the way to a Franco–German 'Zollverein' (customs' union), which would include the common exploitation of the ores of France, Belgium and Luxembourg. This enthusiasm for European unity was, however, mainly confined to the right wing of the party before 1914, more particularly to the group of revisionist intellectuals (Schippel, Calwer, Heine, David, Noske, Quessel and Bernstein), who were connected with the journal *Sozialistische Monatshefte*.

However, it was only with the dreadful destruction wrought by World War I that the notion of European integration, hitherto restricted to intellectual coteries, began to be adopted by really influential political figures. Enthusiasm grew to a peak in the mid-'20s, not only in Germany, but in Western Europe generally. Count Coudenhove-Calergi's *Pan-Europa* and

1

Edo Fimmen's *Labour's Alternative Europe or Europe Ltd'* were two of the most influential catalysts in this enthusiasm.[6] Edo Fimmen's work, a plea for labour to organise on a European level in opposition to the cartels, proved especially influential in the SPD, and a whole spate of books on the theme of European integration were written by SPD authors.[7] This European enthusiasm was fairly widespread, and Breitscheid succeeded in getting a reference to European unity included in the Heidelberg Basic Programme of 1925, the last basic programme of the SPD before the Bad Godesberg Programme of 1959.[8]

> It [the SPD] is in favour of the creation of European economic unity, a unity which has become necessary for economic reasons, and is in favour of the foundation of the United States of Europe, which would bring about the solidarity of the interests of the peoples of the world.

By the late '20s, SPD statements on European integration had become infrequent. The 1929 Year Book merely mentioned in passing the League of Nations' efforts to bring about a European economic rapprochement by means of a tariff armistice.[9] The 1930 Year Book described, but refrained from commenting on, the Briand Memorandum, yet this memorandum from an important European statesman was the major initiative towards European integration in the inter-war period.[10]

The various 'pro-European' pronouncements of the SPD leaders in exile after 1933 reflected an attempt to reconcile their continued belief in internationalism with their claim to be 'good Germans'.[11] The desire to be seen as 'good Germans' sprang from their belief that they would represent the only viable political force in Germany after the inevitable collapse of the Hitler dictatorship — a belief perhaps best expressed by Breitscheid's famous cry 'nach Hitler wir' ('after Hitler, us') of 1933. This made it all the more important that they should not be seen to distance themselves from the fate of the German People. This strain in the policy of the SPD leaders is already evident in the January programme of the Executive in 1934 (the so-called 'Prague Manifesto'), where it is stated that an attempt to use the collapse of the dictatorship in Germany to annex any part of it would be firmly resisted by the SPD.[12]

In general, though, the 'European idea' was primarily invoked as a spiritual value in the first years of the emigration. It represented a belief in the old ideas and values that were identified with Europe. The main goal of the émigrés was the overthrow of the Hitler dictatorship. What Europe would be like after Hitler was a second-order question, though it was taken as self-evident that it would be socialist. In this period Europe was

2

seen as an antithesis to Nazi Germany. This view reappeared very strongly in the ideas of 'Europeans' like Denis de Rougement and Oscar Halecki after 1945.

While the idea of European unity in its various forms was accepted by all the various émigré socialist groups, they were split on the question of the future role of the USSR. The SPD Executive and the majority of moderate socialists were predominantly Western-oriented. The Socialist Workers Party (SAP), International Socialist Combat Group (ISK) and the Neubeginnen Gruppe (NB) were less hostile to the USSR. [13] This division was largely overcome by the signing of the Nazi—Soviet Pact in August 1939. [14]

With the military collapse of France, the SPD Executive was transferred to London, which became the main centre of émigré activity. [15] Much of the early period of the London emigration was taken up in efforts to secure the release from internment of German socialists. There was however a fairly general agreement, reinforced by the fall of France, that the nation-state had become redundant and that some form of European federation was necessary; necessary both for political reasons like the need to contain Germany and for economic reasons. [16]

The German attack on Russia in the summer of 1941 resulted in renewed support for the USSR by the SAP, ISK and NB. [17] Despite this reversion of the socialist splinter groups, they did share many positions with the SPD Executive, and the minutes of a 'Socialist Vanguard Group' meeting in London during Easter 1942 illustrate clearly the issues upon which they were agreed. These were:

1　Europe should no longer be organised on a nation-state basis.
2　There should be no more spheres of influence in Europe.
3　Federal union should be the goal in both politics and economics.
4　A socialist economic and social programme must be produced.
5　An Anglo—US domination of Europe must be prevented.
6　The USSR should not dominate Europe.
7　A socialist Europe would be the best contribution to the security of the USSR.
8　British socialists should support European integration.
9　European politicians, especially socialists, must work for a European future. [18]

By 1943 the memory of the Nazi—Soviet Pact had receded into the background, and even the SPD leadership had modified its hostile attitude towards the USSR and embraced the idea of Europe as a bridge between the capitalist United States and Soviet Russia — a position which had hitherto only been identified with the splinter parties of the left. [19]

In the last years of the War, there was general agreement by leading émigré German socialists with the notion of a democratic, socialist, demilitarised Germany in a democratic, socialist European federation. This provided them with a justification for resisting the attempts of the Allies to annex parts of Germany, and opposing the idea of the collective guilt of the Germans, while enabling them to feel that they were continuing in the internationalist tradition of socialist thought. [20]

Though SPD politicians in exile were primarily concerned with the political organisation of a post-war Europe, they were still socialist enough to believe in the importance of the form of post-war economic system. The fullest picture of their hopes for the post-war economy is to be found in a report of the Economics Committee of all the German Social Democratic Parties in the UK. [21] It envisaged a mixed economy under the overall direction of a 'Central European Economic Committee' and administered on a day-to-day basis by a European Economic Commission. There was provision in this scheme for a coal and steel community, an agricultural authority, central banking and credit institutes, and a monopoly commission. While this plan bore little resemblance to the immediate realities of post-war Europe, it did anticipate the Schuman Plan in its rationale, namely that economic integration was a way of simultaneously creating a European federation and ensuring perpetual peace.

The post-war era 1945—49

This section is concerned with the conditioning factors on the post-war European policy of the SPD. It will, in other words, attempt to explain why the SPD was predisposed to oppose West German participation in a wide range of European institutions, while continuing nevertheless to express many of its traditional views as outlined above.

The most important factor determining the actions of post-war German politicians was the Four-Power occupation of Germany after 1945 and its subsequent division into two hostile camps. Attitudes towards European integration as to everything else were coloured by this situation. The division of Germany into zones of occupation had been arranged even before the end of hostilities, a protocol, signed in London on 12 September 1944, having divided it into three zones. Greater Berlin, regarded as a special case, was also to be divided into three sectors, to be administered jointly by Great Britain, the USA and the USSR. A French occupation zone was created by an additional agreement on 1 May 1945.

4

These arrangements were confirmed in extended form by the Potsdam Agreement of 2 August 1945, when the Oder–Neisse line was recognised to be the provisional border of Germany until the negotiation of a final peace-treaty. The Potsdam Agreement specified that Germany was to be treated as a single economic unit during the occupation period. In theory, supreme authority was vested in the Allied Control Council which met in Berlin. It consisted of the four Commanders-in-chief (whose decisions had to be unanimous), assisted by the political advisers and by directorates corresponding to ministerial departments. France, however, was hostile to even the slightest suggestion of a unified German state and vetoed the creation of any centralised German authorities.

After March 1946, the Control Council gradually ceased to function. In the Four-Power talks of April–May and June–July 1946, and March–April and November 1947, the economic unity and central administration of Germany were still discussed in terms of the Potsdam Agreement. However, two factors were working towards a progressive fusion of the three Western zones. These factors were the steadily worsening state of East–West relations and the need, especially in the British view, to make Western Germany economically sound. On 29 May 1947, the first German Economic Council was created for the combined British and American zones – the so-called 'Economic Council of the Bi-zone'. This was followed by the publication, on 8 January 1948, of the Frankfurt Charter, which established, for the Anglo–US zone, a measure of German participation in government of their economy. The Russians responded to this step on 10 March 1948 by granting the East German Economic Commission broader powers.

During the first London Conference (23 February to 9 March 1948) between representatives of Great Britain, France and the Benelux countries, the French strongly opposed the Anglo–US proposal for a strong central West German government within a federal state. Between sessions of the conference the situation changed rapidly. On 17 March France signed the Brussels Pact which created the Western European Union. On 20 March Marshal Sokolovsky, the Soviet Military Governor, walked out of the Allied Control Council. The Russians began the blockade of West Berlin on 30 March. On 13 April, the US Senate ratified the Marshall Plan Treaty. All these events strengthened the determination of the Western Allies to turn Germany as quickly as possible into a reliable ally.

Thus when the conference reconvened on 20 April 1948, it was concerned primarily with the task of setting up a West German government. The French were prepared to agree to this provided that they were given control of the Saar and provided also that some attempt was made to

5

control the industries of the Ruhr. The final decision of the London Conference, published on 28 December 1948, created the International Authority of the Ruhr (IAR) and authorised it to divide the Ruhr's production of coal, coke and steel between German consumption and export, and to prevent discriminatory practices by the German authorities.

The Minister Presidents of the Länder, who had been asked to arrange for the drafting of a constitution for the new West German State, agreed on 6 July 1948, to call a parliamentary council to draft a 'Basic Law'. Opinion in the Parliamentary Council can be very crudely categorised as being divided between the Centralists (SPD and the Free Democratic Party) and the Federalists (Christian Democrats). The Allies, under French pressure, rejected various German drafts on the grounds that they were too centralistic. The SPD Congress in Hanover (19–20 April 1949) tested the determination of the Allies by approving a constitution which envisaged a more centralised administration. The Foreign Ministers, in their Washington meeting of April 1949, made several concessions in this direction, and on 23 May the military governors finally approved the 'Basic Law'. With this approval the new West German State was virtually established, to be followed on 30 May 1949, by the creation of an East German State.

The SPD's response to post-war developments and its later opposition to European integration, can be explained by the very high proportion of refugees in the party. Fifty out of 131 SPD deputies in the first Bundestag were refugees.[22] These refugees were from areas where the SPD had derived much of its pre-war strength. Before the war areas east of the Elbe had returned a consistent 34 per cent plurality for the SPD,[23] which was therefore much more likely to see reunification as the primary political goal than the largely Catholic CDU/CSU, of which only fifteen out of 139 deputies in the first Bundestag were refugees.[24]

This factor assumes even greater significance when one considers how many SPD leaders had been exiles or had been otherwise persecuted during the Nazi regime.[25] Their primary concern, sometimes characterised as émigré neurosis, was to assert their national identity with the German people, rather than to strive to be on good terms with the Allies who had made possible their return to Germany. In practical politics this again involved the stressing of the reunification issue. Moreover, the absence of the guilt feelings that inhibited other German parties in their relations with the Allies, and the greater experience of its leading politicians, meant that the SPD displayed more self-confidence in presenting these ideas.[26] This assertiveness turned in many cases to disillusionment with and bitterness to the Allied authorities and their policies when the Western Allies, as

6

often happened, failed to choose SPD supporters to run the new Germany.

If we take the Allied occupation of Germany and its subsequent division as constituting the framework within which German politics were carried on, then the crucial factor in determining the SPD position was the emergence of Kurt Schumacher at the Kloster Wennigsen conference of October 1945, as the first post-war leader of the party.

> Until a stroke in December 1951, removed him from the scene eight months before his death, he dominated the leadership both in and out of parliament. . .

> There was later absolutely no doubt in the minds of Schumacher's closest associates that he made every major decision affecting the national policy of his party between 1946 and 1952. [27]

Kurt Schumacher was born at Kulm near Danzig, in the area known as the 'Grenzdeutschtum' and traditionally associated with national consciousness in Germany. His place of origin has also been accounted a reason for his marked anti-clericalism, which made him very suspicious of the motives of the three Allied High Commissioners, McLoy, François Poncet and Kirkpatrick, who were all Catholics. [28] In this connection, he stood in direct contrast to Konrad Adenauer, his main political rival, who was the scion of an old Rhenish Catholic family, and the inheritor, therefore, of an explicitly Catholic French oriented strain in German policy. [29]

Schumacher always possessed a strong national consciousness and fought as a volunteer in the First World War. Shortly after the end of it he completed his Doctoral dissertation, 'Der Kampf um den Staatsgedanken in der deutschen Sozialdemokratie' (Münster 1926), in which he acknowledged his debt to Ferdinand Lasalle, Karl Renner, J. Plenge, and H. Cunow, rather than to the more international tradition of socialist thought represented by Marx and Kautsky. Schumacher felt that he belonged to the Jaurès tradition of socialist thought. He constantly recommended his works to young socialists and made the same distinction between 'national' (patriotic) and 'nationalistisch' (aggressive) nationalism. [30] In post-war Germany this national consciousness meant that German reunification rather than Western European integration was regarded by him as the primary goal.

Schumacher's speeches mirrored the ideas developed by the SPD members who had been in exile. [31] It was an ambivalent mixture of nationalism tempered by a continuing commitment to socialist internationalism. This combination is well expressed in a speech made in January 1946.

For the SPD there is no fictitious fatherland of labour. For us Social Democrats there is the German homeland which we wish to hold together as a governmental, national and economic whole. Our policy is at the same time and with equal justification national and international. We can envisage Europe only as an association of truly free peoples. [32]

This nationalist strain in his view offered some chance of appealing to the huge number of refugees in West Germany who might otherwise be attracted to a new totalitarian movement. [33] It would also prevent the SPD from being identified with a policy of fulfilment. Although he was later often to use the demand for 'Gleichberechtigung' (parity of rights) as a tactical weapon there is little doubt that he genuinely believed in it as a pre-condition for action at the international level, without which the most likely result would be the creation of aggressive nationalism. Unlike Adenauer, he believed that the exigencies of the Cold War would force the Western Allies to grant this 'Gleichberechtigung' in return for German support. A popular nationalist policy would, he felt, give the SPD some hope of breaking out of its traditional minority position. This nationalism was in no danger of being outbid from the right since any extreme nationalist groups were likely to be outlawed either by the German courts or directly by the Allies. It also had the advantage of distinguishing the SPD from the KPD, who, while pursuing an opposition line on foreign policy, were seen by Schumacher as agents of a foreign power.

Paradoxically, then, Schumacher's strategy involved safeguarding democracy in Germany and preventing the emergence of a totalitarian national movement by an emphasis on German national rights. 'The task is to make nationalism impossible by upholding national rights.' [34]

Since all real power lay with the occupation authorities this normally meant opposition to their policies. Schumacher had a vivid sense of history and was haunted by the identification of the SPD with a policy of fulfilment in the Weimar Republic. He therefore made the fateful decision in the summer of 1947, to go into opposition in the Frankfurt Economic Council, confident that this would bring long-term benefits to the SPD.

Schumacher's relations with other countries were conditioned by these views, which were normally coloured more by his nationalism than by his socialist internationalism. His nationalism meant that he was anti-French as well as anti-Russian: 'For Schumacher's socialist nationalist policy the most dangerous enemies were France and the USSR'. [35] This Francophobia was based partly on recollections of French conduct in the Ruhr in 1923, but mainly on French post-war actions, especially the annexation of the Saar, which he saw as damaging to German unity.[36] France had opposed central agencies for Germany in 1947 and the establishment of a centralised German government in the Staatenbund-*versus*-Bundesstaat controversy. Schumacher never visited France, and had very poor relations with André François Poncet, the French High Commissioner and erstwhile appeasing Ambassador in the Nazi period.[37]

This suspicion of France was shared by many SPD supporters, because Vichy France had handed over to the Nazis, under the terms of the Armistice clause of 1940, many SPD refugees, including Rudolf Breitscheid and Rudolf Hilferding. Many officers and officials of the French occupation forces had been identified with Vichy. Relations with French socialists, particularly with Jules Moch and to a lesser extent with Guy Mollet, were very bad and defied all Salamon Grumbach's attempts at mediation. Schumacher was incensed by the French Socialist attitude during the constitutional crisis, when the SFIO supported the more federal (Staatenbund) plan for West Germany.[38]

However, relations with Britain and Scandinavian countries where many SPD members had spent their exile were reasonably good. The British Labour Party had been the only socialist party to deal directly with the SPD in exile, and the British were the first to allow the re-establishment of political parties in the Western zones. This took place on 6 August 1945, and was generally considered to be to the SPD's advantage.

It was to Britain that Schumacher made his first official journey abroad in 1946, but closer relations between the SPD and the Labour Party were frustrated by a certain anti-German strain, particularly marked in Dalton, but also apparent in some of Bevin's policies. The SPD also felt let down by Britain's abandonment of its earlier support for the nationalisation of the heavy industries of the Ruhr. Despite these tensions, which were mainly on the British side, a Europe without Britain was anathema to Schumacher. Since the Labour government displayed little enthusiasm for European unity at that time, Schumacher's attitude was necessarily reserved, especially since the moves towards European integration that the British government supported at that time (the Dunkirk Treaty of 1947 and the Brussels Pact) were directed nominally at least against the danger of a renascent Germany.

Since we have now established Schumacher's general views it is possible to deal more precisely with his views on European unity. In the period in which we are interested, two successive views of Europe can be isolated. In the first period, 1945–47, Schumacher saw a neutralised Germany playing a major role in a Europe organised on a classical balance of power lines.

9

The SPD's interest lies in the greatest possible co-operation between the Great Powers and it will therefore, endorse a policy of compromise and balance of power. It recognises that the vitally necessary European economic unity requires the creation of corresponding political institutions . . . . A European framework based on the balance of power will never function properly unless Germany as a whole is incorporated into it. [39]

In Schumacher's opinion a unilateral pro-Russian orientation as suggested by Grotewohl could only disturb this balance of power. In the period 1947—48, he was attracted to the idea of Europe as a third force, as a bloc of west and central European socialist states. [40]

Europe will either find its own lines of development or it will be crushed between two giant millstones. The Russians must recognise that Europe must be democratic in order to be European, and the United States must recognise that the alternative to socialism in Europe is Dictatorship. [41]

However, in the course of time he had to recognise that socialism was not going to triumph all over Europe, and that the British attitude to any form of genuine integration was distinctly reserved. This realisation hardened his attitude towards European integration. Nevertheless, while his policy on Europe was often contradictory, two basic premises remained constant: 'that any European solution which rested on German division was essentially anti-European and that the future sovereignty of Germany could only be given up to a European organisation which accorded Germany parity of rights and esteem'. [42]

Despite his great stress on reunification and also, in the early years, on a European balance of power, his loyalty towards the West, due to his bitter anti-communism, was never really in doubt. He welcomed the Marshall Plan for example, though he added that the European Recovery Programme (ERP) must not hinder the establishment of socialism. He was particularly well disposed to the Marshall Plan after the Antwerp meeting of Comisco (the first post-war grouping of social democratic parties) in November/December 1947, when it was decided to have a meeting of all socialist parties to work out a common policy on the Marshall Plan. Schumacher felt that the SPD had attained 'Gleichberechtigung' in Marshall Plan questions at a time when the government of the Western zones was in the hands of the Allied High Commissioners.

10

Conflict and consensus within the party, 1945–49

Although, with the possible exception of Bebel, Schumacher was the monocratic leader *par excellence* in the history of the SPD, his views on European unity did not command universal support in the party. Schumacher's support lay essentially with the functionaries, the organisation men, Willi Eichler, Erich Ollenhauer, Fritz Heine and Alfried Nau, economists like Dr Agartz, and the party activists. Carlo Schmid, a possible rival, quarrelled with Schumacher in 1948 and early 1949, but was to be one of his strongest supporters during the rest of Schumacher's lifetime.

Schumacher's power derived ultimately from the moral authority he had earned by his courageous resistance to Nazism in the last days of Weimar and in Dachau. It was anchored in his dual position as Chairman of the Party Executive (Vorstand) and the Parliamentary Party (Fraktion). The Party Executive was elected by the delegates at the Party Conference. Schumacher and three or four other salaried members of the Committee formed the Acting Executive Committee (Geschäftsführende Vorstand). The Acting Executive Committee carried on the daily business of the national party organisation and represented the party in between congresses.

The authority of the Party Executive had been weakened in comparison with the Weimar period by making the district secretary an employee of the local organisation rather than the National Executive. The political neutralisation of the trade unions also made it very dependent on the dues collected by local organisations. On the other hand, the position of the Party Executive *vis-à-vis* the Congress was strengthened by the post-war provision that the Congress only met bi-annually.

The Party Executive was formally accountable to the Party Congress and the Party Committee (Parteiausschuss), which consisted of representatives of the regional district organisations. The Party Executive was supposed to summon this group four times a year to discuss important party problems, and in addition the Control Commission (Kontrollkomission) elected by the Party Congress was in theory supposed to keep a close eye on the Executive's conduct of party affairs. In fact, all these groups, and especially the Party Congress, were fairly unwieldy, and during Schumacher's lifetime his dominant position, based ultimately on his unshakeable moral authority, was never seriously challenged.

Schumacher's use of his moral authority as a resource not only to sustain his leadership but in general policy discussions led him to overreact to internal opposition to his policies. One of the recurring themes in the following chapters will be the contrast between Schumacher's generally shrewd appreciation of a general political situation, and his insensitive handling of allies and those who disagreed with him in the party.

Opposition to Schumacher was grouped around the so-called 'Bürgermeisterflügel' of the SPD, the Länder politicians. Though small in number, this group was rich in prestige and experience, including as it did men like Ernst Reuter, Max Brauer, Wilhelm Kaisen, and Wilhelm Hoegner. These men in power in the regions were conditioned by different factors. Unlike Schumacher, they were prepared to go into coalition governments, because their primary interest was in local and regional problems of reconstruction. They held that the solution of these problems required co-operation with the bourgeois parties and the occupation authorities. [43] Co-operation with the Allies was a *sine qua non* for Reuter and also for Kaisen: Bremen was the port for the US zone. Schumacher had, as noted above, taken the view that too close an identification with Allied policies would be electorally disastrous, and had gone into opposition as early as 1947. These regional leaders benefited from the dramatic change in Allied policy towards Germany in 1948 as the Cold War intensified. This was particularly important for Reuter in Berlin, because of Allied help against the Soviet blockade, but was also true in varying degrees for the other leaders, as the Allies (especially the Americans) poured money into West Germany under the Marshall Plan.

The general position adopted by these regional leaders seemed better adapted to post-1945 German realities than Schumacher's posture of opposition. Nearly all observers have commented on what Kirchheimer has called 'the privatisation of German life', meaning a concentration on individual advancement and neglect of public questions. [44] Votes generally went to the party which best succeeded in maximising economic welfare, rather than the party with a more coherent ideology.

By and large, these leaders were more cosmopolitan than Schumacher. All of them had very good contacts with the United States, whose government provided much of the impetus for post-war attempts at European integration. Reuter also had very good contacts with Britain and France. [45] They were idealistic Europeans in a way that Schumacher was not. Most of them had joined MSEUE, the Socialist Movement for the United States of Europe, in 1947. Kaisen took part in the Hague Congress for the United States of Europe in 1948, though the SPD did not officially attend. [46]

These men were 'Grosse Persönlichkeiten' in their own districts, although Kurt Schumacher tried continually to minimise their influence in the party. In Berlin, for example, the SPD, in contrast to the national organisation, was a 'voters' party, dependent therefore on strong public personalities. The CDU in Berlin, like the national SPD, was a 'members' party, dependent for its appeal on an alternative programme.[47] These men were thus in a position to oppose the line taken by Schumacher. This was not so for ordinary deputies who were too dependent on the party list (owing to the paucity of safe seats), to make opposition either likely or profitable. Their opposition to Schumacher was limited by the need to take into account the views of the local party members and parliamentary deputies, which were usually identical with those of the Party Executive, and an uneasy *modus vivendi* was arrived at in which they agreed not to press this disagreement too far. As in most modern disciplined parties, dissent was expressed primarily at conferences and more rarely in the Executive. However, apart from the two areas of European integration and federal-state relations the 'Bürgermeisterflügel' never really operated as a group.

Carlo Schmid also distanced himself at this time from Schumacher's stance on Europe, though to speak of this as opposition would be to exaggerate. He was just a novice in a party where the great majority of the membership had been active before 1933. Unusually for a prominent member of the SPD, he was also a member of the Europa-Union though he saw much more clearly than most of its members that it was not possible to build European unity solely on the basis of a primitive anti-communism. His views on Europe at this time can be expressed in three hypotheses:

> Europe can only fulfill its world-political role as a third power between the two super-powers. This was really a question of power rather than goodwill, and would demand the political organisation of Europe. Germany should remain apart from this integration process until a stage was reached where it could bear the load of a reunified Germany.[48]

The distinction between Schmid and Schumacher is obvious. Schmid did not insist on a socialist Europe though he would naturally prefer it. Although the division of Germany precluded the immediate entry of West Germany into the integration process, the process ought still to be encouraged.[49]

Conclusion

With the qualification introduced by the attitude of the Länder politicians and Carlo Schmid, the SPD position at the time of the establishment of the Federal Republic could thus fairly be represented as one of 'opposition' to the way things were developing. It was too late to oppose the establishment of the free market economy since it was by now a *fait accompli* and opposition was transferred to the field of foreign affairs, primarily against the International Ruhr Authority. The SPD at first refused to co-operate with the CDU, but later they ratified a common protest resolution in the North Rhine–Westphalia Landtag on 11 January 1949. This opposition was based on 'national' grounds, and although Schumacher maintained that the fact that this was carried on by socialists rendered it respectable, it was still nationalism. Schumacher's calculation that this nationalism would appeal to refugees was in fact substantiated.[50] Nevertheless, a price had to be paid for this, and the price was opposition to West German participation in various European institutions.

Notes

[1] E.B. Haas, *The Uniting of Europe, Political, Social and Economic Forces, 1950–57*, London, 1958. In general this is an important and useful book.

[2] See W. Hanrieder, *West German Foreign Policy 1949–63*, Stanford, 1967, for a brilliant examination of West German foreign policy from this prespective.

[3] Haas, op. cit., pp. 131–40.

[4] Otto Kirchheimer, 'The Waning of Opposition in Parliamentary Regimes', *Social Research*, summer 1957, pp. 127–57.

[5] C.R. Rose, 'The relation of socialist principles to British Labour foreign policy, 1945–51', Oxford D.Phil., 1960.

[6] R. Coudenhove-Calergi, *Pan-Europa*, Leipzig 1926; E. Fimmen, *Labour's Alternative Europe or Europe Ltd.*, London 1924.

[7] See in particular Hermann Kranhold, *Vereinigte Staaten Von Europa – eine Aufgabe proletärischer Politik*, Hanover 1924; Otto Lehmann–Russbüldt, *Republik Europa*, Berlin 1925; Wladimir Woytinski, *Die Vereinigten-Staaten Von Europa*, Berlin 1926.

[8] W. Treue, *Deutsche Partei Programme 1861–1951*, Berlin 1954, p. 110.

[9] SPD *Jahrbuch*, 1929, p. 21.

[10] SPD *Jahrbuch*, 1930, pp. 32ff.

[11] See in particular Erich Matthias *Sozialdemokratie und Nation. Ein Beitrag zur Ideengeschichte der sozialdemokratischen Emigration 1933–38*, Stuttgart 1952.

[12] E. Matthias, op. cit., p. 184.

[13] The SAP, ISK and Neubeginnen Gruppe were all small splinter groups made up largely of ex-SPD members, who had quarrelled with the SPD leadership on the tactics to be adopted towards Nazism. Willy Brandt was a member of SAP at this period. A good overview of their aims can be got from the following books: *Die Sozialistische Republik. Der Programm des ISK*, London 1937; Neu Beginnen, *Der Kommende Weltkrieg. Aufgaben und Ziele des deutschen Sozialismus*, Paris-Selbstverlag des Verfassers, 1939; *Neu Beginnen — Was es will, was es ist and wie es würde*, Auslandsbüro, Neu Beginnen, London 1939.

[14] See Dr W. Röder, *Die Deutschen Sozialistischen Exilgruppen in Gross—britannien 1940—45*, Hanover 1968. Röder gives a very full description of the activities of all the exile socialist groups.

[15] I shall therefore concentrate on the plans produced in London. The ideas of the SPD emigration in the USA were very similar to those in London. See Michael Kuehl, 'Die Exilierte Deutsche Demokratische Linke in USA', *Zeitschrift für Politik* 1957, pp. 274—89. Heinrich Ritzel, who was in exile in Switzerland, took a more idealistic, more utopian, less nationalistic line than those members who were in belligerent countries. In his first book, written with H. Bauer, *Von der eidgenössischen zur europäischen Föderation*, Zurich 1940, he advanced the idea of a European unity on the Swiss model. His later books occasionally vary in their emphasis on one detail or another, but the basic plan remains the same.

[16] See G. Luetkens, *A New Order for Germany*, London 1941.

[17] See W. Röder, op. cit., p. 108; Paul Walter, *Sozialistische Revolution gegen Nazi-Imperialismus, zur Politik der Sozialistischen Arbeiter-Partei*, SAP Ortsgruppe, London, February 1943.

[18] Socialist Vanguard Group, *Calling all Europe*, London 1942. These views were very widely held: see for instance, Willi Eichler *et al*, *Towards European Unity; Franco—German Relations*, ISK, London 1943.

[19] *Vorstellungen über die Sozial Demokratie in Deutschland nach dem Sturz der Hitler-Diktatur*, Londoner Vertretung der SPD, June 1943.

[20] This position was opposed by Curt Geyer, a prominent member of the SPD in exile who became a proponent of Lord Vansittart's views and resigned his position as member of the SPD Executive in Exile in January 1942, in order to establish a 'Fight for Freedom Committee'. Although Geyer had some influence with the Labour Party, he had very little effect on the SPD's position. Cf. Curt Geyer, *Gollancz in German Wonderland*, London 1942.

[21] W. Fliess, *The Economic Reconstruction of Europe*, ISK, London 1944.

[22] Alfred Grosser, *La Démocratie de Bonn*, Paris 1958, p. 99.

[23] Ibid.

[24] Ibid.

[25] Ibid.

[26] R. Wildenmann, *Partei und Fraktion — ein Beitrag zur Analyse der Politischen Willensbildung und des Parteiensystems in der Bundesrepublik*, Meisenheim am Glan 1954, p. 16; also L. Bergstrasser, *Geschichte der Politischen Parteien in Deutschland*, Munich 1960, p. 324.

[27] L. Edinger, *Kurt Schumacher — a Study in Personality and Political Behaviour*, London 1965, pp. 112—17.

[28] Interview with Schumacher's confidant Arno Scholz, editor of *Der Telegraf.* In the same interview Scholz said that Schumacher regarded Adenauer as a 'Ritter der Katholischen Kirche' (knight of the Catholic Church).

[29] On Adenauer's pro-French proclivities see especially K.D. Erdmann, *Adenauer in der Rheinlandpolitik nach dem ersten Weltkrieg*, Stuttgart 1966.

[30] Waldemar Ritter, *Kurt Schumacher, Eine Untersuchung seiner politischen Konzeption und seiner Gesellschafts und Staatsauffassung*, Hanover 1964, p. 109.

[31] I have talked over this point with Fritz Heine, Willi Eichler and Erwin Schoettle and all three pointed out how amazed they were by the closeness of Schumacher's views to those they had developed in exile.

[32] Cited in F. Wesemann, *Kurt Schumacher — ein Leben für Deutschland*, Frankfurt 1952, p. 98.

[33] L. Edinger, op. cit., p. 81. For a similar view on the refugees, see S. Neumann, 'The new crisis strata in German society' in H. Morgenthau (ed.) *Germany and the Future of Europe*, Chicago 1950, pp. 25—50.

[34] K. Schumacher, 'Die Sozialdemokratie im Kampf um Deutschland und Europa', *Protokoll der Verhandlungen des Parteitages der SPD*, Hamburg 1950, p. 83.

[35] Theo Pirker, *Die SPD nach Hitler — Die Geschichte der Sozialdemokratischen Partei Deutschlands, 1945—1964*, Munich 1965, p. 44.

[36] L. Edinger, op. cit., p. 46.

[37] K. Boelling, *Republic in Suspense*, Pall Mall, London 1964, p. 97.

[38] A. Grosser, *Die Bonner Demokratie*, Bonn 1960, pp. 138—9.

[39] K. Schumacher's speech at the Kloster Wennigsen Conference, October 1945, cited in Hans Peter Schwarz, *Vom Reich zur Bundesrepublik — Deutschland im Widerstreit der aussenpolitischen Konzeptionen in den Jahren der Besatzungsherrschaft 1945—49*, Berlin 1966, p. 200.

[40] Cf. note 19 above.

[41] Frankfurt, June 1947, SPD Vorstands-Archiv, Bonn.

[42] Kurt Schumacher, *Nach dem Zusammenbruch*, 1946, pp. 133, 176.

[43] Brauer and Kaisen owed their initial appointments to the Allies. Reuter was a party nominee, but the special position of Berlin involved dependence on the Western Allies. On Reuter's emergence see P. Windsor, *Berlin, City on Leave*, London 1963. On Kaisen, see his autobiography, *Meine Arbeit, mein Leben*, Munich 1967. My information on Max Brauer is based on an extended interview with him in 1966.

[44] O. Kirchheimer, 'Notes on the political scene in Western Germany', p. 205 in *Politics, Law and Social Change*, selected essays of Otto Kirchheimer, Burin and Shell (ed.) London 1969.

[45] On Reuter's policy also see A. Ashkenasi, *Reformpartei und Aussenpolitik — Die Aussenpolitik der SPD*, Berlin, Bonn, Cologne 1968.

[46] W. Kaisen, *Meine Arbeit, mein Leben*, Munich 1967, pp. 380—8.

[47] P. Windsor, op. cit., p. 162.

[48] H. Schwarz, op. cit., p. 574.

[49] This nuanced difference between Schmid and Schumacher is very clear in a speech by Schmid to the German Section of the Europa-Union, where he welcomed the Council of Europe. See C. Schmid, *Deutschland und der europäische Rat — Schriftenreihe des Deutschen Rates der europäischen Bewegung* 1949. Willy Brandt, by this time Ernst Reuter's chief lieutenant, had taken a line similar to Schmidt's general position in his first speech before an SPD Party Conference. Parteitag der SPD 1948, Düsseldorf, Protokoll, p. 59.

[50] During Schumacher's period of leadership the SPD did particularly well in areas like Schleswig-Holstein, which contained a high proportion of refugees.

2 Opposition to West German Participation in the IAR and Council of Europe

Background

The return of Kurt Schumacher to active politics in April 1949, following a long illness, coincided with the beginning of the election campaign for the first German Bundestag. The campaign itself largely revolved round economic issues. Under the aegis of Professor Erhard industrial production had risen from 54 per cent of the 1936 level in January 1948 to 84 per cent in February 1949. The SPD maintained that this increase was illusory and held that the increase in unemployment from 450,000 to 1,300,000 during the same period was much the more significant figure.[1] Schumacher knew little of economics, however, and relied very heavily on the advice of Professors Baade and Nölting and Doctor Agartz, especially Professor Nölting.[2]

During the campaign Schumacher made a disastrous tactical mistake in a speech at Gelsenkirchen on 22 June 1949, when he said, 'We shall not knuckle under either to a French General or to a Roman Cardinal ... we respect the Church, but we are determined not to subject the German people to a fifth occupying power.'[3] Schumacher's attack, skilfully exploited by the CDU, which had been on the defensive after Schumacher's success in the constitutional crisis of April 1949, left Catholic workers little alternative but to vote CDU. In the event, the CDU/CSU emerged as the strongest party, polling 7·36 million votes as against the SPD's 6·95 million.

There is wide disagreement among writers on this period as to whether or not Schumacher had in fact expected to win. Lewis Edinger maintains that Schumacher expected the election to result in the splitting up of the 'Bürgerblock', an eventuality which would allow him to form either a weakly-opposed minority government or a coalition incorporating some minor parties and perhaps even some left-wing CDU members like Karl Arnold.[4] Theo Pirker, in contrast, holds that Schumacher had assumed that the SPD would probably be unable to form an absolute majority and

19

that the Bürgerblock would hold together.[5] He bases this belief on the SPD conduct of the campaign. During the campaign the SPD had present-ed itself as an opposition party rather than as a potential governing party. This seems to me to correspond more to the logic of the Schumacher 'opposition course', a policy which, as we saw in Chapter 1, he had favour-ed since 1947.

Immediately after the election there was a great deal of speculation about a possible 'grand coalition' between the CDU and the SPD. A number of leading personalities in both parties, largely Länder politicians like Karl Arnold of North Rhine–Westphalia, Minister President Altmeier of the Rhineland Palatinate, Werner Hilpert of Hesse and Guenter Gereke of Lower Saxony in the CDU, and Paul Löbe (Berlin), Max Brauer (Hamburg) and Wilhelm Kaisen (Bremen) of the SPD were in favour of such a course. Coalition was, however, always extremely unlikely, given the personal antipathy between Adenauer and Schumacher and Schuma-cher's conception of 'opposition'. Adenauer in fact ruled out any possibil-ity of coalition by calling a meeting of leading CDU/CSU politicians at his house in Rhöndorf on 21 August 1949. Although, according to Adenau-er's own testimony, the partisans of coalition were very determined, he succeeded in dissuading them by emphasising the differences on economic policy between the two parties.[6] He was greatly helped in this by the absence of Karl Arnold and the early departure of Werner Hilpert, who lacking a car of his own had to leave early.[7]

Fritz Heine had already made the position of the protagonists of coali-tion well nigh impossible by declaring on election night, on behalf of the SPD, that possession of the Economics Ministry would be a minimum condition for SPD participation in a CDU-led coalition — a condition which was known to be unacceptable to the CDU/CSU leadership.[8]

Schumacher had in any case announced immediately the results were known that the SPD policy would be one of intransigent opposition.[9] This policy was based on the belief that, given the small majority enjoyed by the CDU-led coalition, it would be able to administer but not to govern, and would need SPD support to carry out any major measures. The SPD would therefore be able to exert most influence by a policy of intransigence. The Party Executive met in Bad Dürkheim from 29 to 30 August 1949 to work out future policy. It produced a series of resolutions described characteristically by Schumacher as the 'Dokument der Opposi-tion'. These resolutions were formulated by Schumacher and a group of close colleagues, namely Carlo Schmid, Willi Eichler, Otto Suhr, Waldemar von Knoeringen and Erwin Schoettle. These resolutions proved to be atypical of the actual conduct of opposition since, of the sixteen resolutions, only three could be construed as affecting foreign policy. These resolutions were nos. 11, 13 and 16. Resolution 11 called for restriction of Allied interference in German affairs, an alteration of the Ruhr Statute and an end to the dismantling of German industries concerned with the production of goods for peaceful use. Resolution 13 demanded the rejection of the Oder–Neisse as Germany's Eastern Border, the continuation of the Saar as part of the German State, and resistance to any new territorial demands. According to resolution 16, the SPD was fighting for the equality of all peoples and a new order for Europe, while at the same time rejecting any form of nationalism. For this reason the SPD would fight for the reunification of Germany on the basis of personal and political freedom in all the occupied zones, especially the Soviet zone.[10]

More important than the precise content of the resultions, was the style of opposition established by Schumacher at Bad Dürkheim. Opposition, in Schumacher's view, demanded a clear programme and constant initiatives – a policy which has been characterised by Pirker as Schumacher's 'as if' policy – that is, carrying on the opposition as if he were the government, though this would be regarded by an Anglo–American political scientist as more like the normal policy of an opposition.[11]

Schumacher, in a declaration at this meeting, set the tone for SPD opposition.

> The political role of the opposition in the state has still to be made clear to the Germans. Let the watchword of the SPD be to act as a decisive force and not to compromise or accept the responsibility for acts carried out by others.[12]

These decisions were approved by a small party conference at Cologne on 6 September 1949.[13] This procedure was extensively used during the Schumacher years (a small conference consisted of the Party Executive, the Party Committee, Control Commission, Parliamentary Party and the Minister Presidents of SPD-governed Länder).

Schumacher's first demonstration of his 'opposition course' came during the election of the Federal President. The CDU/FDP coalition were backing Theodor Heuss. Some CDU leaders opposed his candidature and proposed instead that the SPD be given at least nominal responsibility by electing a moderate Social Democrat like Louise Schröder, Max Brauer or Paul Löbe. There was fairly wide support for such a policy in the SPD, but Schumacher insisted that he himself contest the office in order to prevent the election of one of these figures, which would imply SPD co-responsibility. Heuss in fact failed to obtain a majority in the first ballot, but defeated Schumacher (he obtained 416 votes to Schumacher's 312) in the second.[14] It is tempting to speculate on the situation that would have been produced had Adenauer overcome his antipathy to Schumacher and instructed his party to vote for Schumacher. Schumacher would then either have been forced to accept the co-responsibility he feared, or turn down the office with disastrous loss of face.

Schumacher's belief that the coalition was very weak was apparently confirmed when three days later Adenauer was elected Chancellor by the margin of one vote – his own! Adenauer very firmly rejected the idea of coalition in his opening declaration on the 20 September 1949, and justified the idea of 'opposition' in almost the same terms as Schumacher. While he agreed with Schumacher's rejection of the Oder–Neisse line as the definitive German border, he saw the solution to German difficulties, particularly in relation to the Saar, in a European Union.[15]

Schumacher made use of his opening speech to put forward his idea of opposition.

> The opposition cannot be expected to function as a substitute party for the government and to accept responsibility for acts which many government parties would be reluctant to endorse. Opposition is an important part of the life of the state and not a second-rank auxiliary for the government. *The essence of opposition is a permanent attempt to force the government and its parties, by concrete proposals tuned to concrete situations, to pursue the political line outlined by the opposition.*[16]

On the question of European integration Schumacher's position was diametrically opposed to Adenauer. The legal claim to the Saar, which had been separated from Germany in 1946, must be preserved at all costs to avoid weakening the German people's enthusiasm for international cooperation. Europe could only be built on the basis of equality.[17]

The opposition to West German participation in the IAR

The first clash between government and opposition on foreign affairs came over the question of West German entry into the International Ruhr Authority (IAR). The positions taken and arguments employed, particularly on the issue of West German sovereignty, foreshadowed the later more important debates about entry into European institutions.

The IAR had grown out of the London Conference of the three occupying powers in West Germany and the Benelux countries in the early summer of 1948. In line with her traditional policy, France had demanded international control of the Ruhr production and military guarantees of her own security if a West German state were to be created. Unable to get the support of even the Benelux countries, the French were forced to accept a compromise solution. This compromise solution involved an agreement in principle on the creation of an International Ruhr Authority to control the distribution of the Ruhr's coal, coke and steel products. The United States, Great Britain, France, the Benelux countries and Germany were to be represented on the authority, though Germany's vote was to be cast by the Allied High Commissioners. [18]

When the Conference reconvened in November, inter-Allied relations had been badly strained by the action of the Bi-zonal authorities, who had promulgated Military Government Law no. 75 on the re-organisation of the German coal, iron and steel industries on 10 November. The French government was particularly enraged by the preamble which stated that the 'military government has decided that the question of the eventual ownership of the coal, iron and steel industries should be left to the determination of a freely elected German government', since they rightly saw this as taking an important lever of influence out of their hands. They were, however, largely placated by being invited to sit on the 'Essen Groups', the Bi-zonal committees charged with supervising the German administration of Ruhr coal and steel industries.

The final decisions of the London Conference, published on 28 December 1948, officially created the International Ruhr Authority and authorised it to divide the Ruhr's coal, coke and steel products between German consumption and exports. Provision was also made to prevent discriminatory practices by the German authorities. The important decision on control of German administration in the Ruhr was postponed until the end of the military government period. Powers of supervision already exercised by the coal and steel groups would be transferred to the IAR or the Military Security Board only if it were necessary to ensure 'that the general policies and general programmes relating to production development and investment in these industries are in conformity with the purposes stated in the preamble'. Another meeting was held in London from 20 May to 2 June 1948, and the International Ruhr Authority was formally installed in Düsseldorf on 6 August 1949.

A Military Security Board was set up parallel to the International Ruhr Authority to 'ensure the maintenance of disarmament and demilitarisation in the interests of security and carry out the proper inspections and to make the necessary recommendations to the military government, who decide the action to be taken'. Agreement was reached on the organisation of this body on 17 December 1948, and its creation was announced by the three Foreign Ministers on 17 January 1949. Its responsibility was to prevent the revival of military and para-military organisations and of war production or militarily useful scientific research, as well as enforcing the prohibition of specific types of industrial production. The first German reaction to the IAR, in 1948, had been uniformly hostile. Konrad Adenauer had attempted to build a united German front against the decisions of the London Conference. To this end, in company with Dr Süsterhenn, he met Ollenhauer, Heine and Fritz Henssler on 17 June 1948. [19] Although the SPD was also opposed to the establishment of an International Ruhr Authority, the party leadership was unwilling to adopt a common position — partly on obvious tactical grounds, but mainly because Schumacher was very ill. During Schumacher's various illnesses, the salaried members of the Executive, 'the apparatchiki', were very reluctant to act in any way which might tie Schumacher's hands in the future. Some co-operation was achieved later and the SPD, CDU, FDP and the Zentrumspartei adopted a common protest motion in the North Rhine—Westphalia Landtag on 11 January 1949.

After his accession to the office of Chancellor, Adenauer reversed his previous posture of 'opposition'. Although he lacked the necessary constitutional powers to carry on a foreign policy, Adenauer was in fact able to function fairly effectively through the medium of negotiations with the High Commissioners and by press interviews. Adenauer was in a fairly strong position, since Allied policy towards Germany had been in something of a cleft stick since 1948. While tremendous efforts were being made through the Marshall Plan and other agencies to rebuild Germany industrially, dismantling continued. Adenauer's view was that while the International Ruhr Authority really belonged more to the tradition of dismantling, of keeping Germany in check, than to the efforts to promote German industrial expansion, West Germany could safely join it, since events were working to change the status quo in West Germany's favour.

Adenauer concentrated first on ensuring that his Cabinet shared his change of heart. At a meeting of the Cabinet on 25 October 1949, he stated that entry into the Ruhr Authority would bring foreign policy benefits. Intransigence on the other hand would be met with intransigence on the Allied side, and this at a time when the Ruhr was desperately in need of American capital. No trouble was anticipated from the trade unions, since it was known that Hans Böckler, the chairman of the DGB and a fellow native of Cologne, was in favour of German entry. [20]

Adenauer's view was strengthened by an interview with General Robertson on the 31 October 1949. Robertson, who had just seen Bevin, indicated that a proposal to strike works off the dismantling list, or to make substitutions as the Minister of Economic Affairs (Erhard) had suggested, had not the slightest chance of success. There was a possibility of 'breaking through the ring', however, and this was to treat dismantling not as an economic problem, but from the standpoint of the security needs of the Western Allies. The Federal Republic must recognise this need by withdrawing its previous refusal to co-operate in the Military Security Board and by sending a member to the Ruhr Authority. [21]

Adenauer made his position public in an extensive interview on 7 November 1949 to the American newspaper *The Baltimore Sun*, a newspaper known by him to be regularly read by President Truman. In this interview, he advanced the view that French security needs in Germany could be met by allowing the French to invest up to 40 per cent in German industries, especially the steel industry. The United States was to provide the money for French investment. The improvement of Franco—German relations was to be the core of this policy. He ended by saying that 'we shall soon be prepared to join the Ruhr Commission', without naming a date, but indicating that he regarded the cessation of dismantling as a favourable moment. [22] This interview was calculated by Adenauer mainly to influence the Foreign Ministers' Conference which was to meet at Paris on 9 November.

Schumacher was incensed by the Adenauer interview, which he regarded as a betrayal of the German position, and he gave a series of intransigent interviews on 9, 10, 11 and 12 November. [23] The question of the Ruhr Authority had been mentioned but not fully discussed in the Parliamentary Party. Schumacher had mentioned a communist request for a common front on the Ruhr Authority, which it was decided to reject at a Parliamentary Party meeting on the 22 September. [24] The Parliamentary Party had, however, been unable to formulate a precise position on the question of entry, though it was understood that the choice lay between a negative vote and an abstention should there be a debate. [25] The SPD position in general was based on the resolution of the Socialist International Conference of 7 June 1948, especially the penultimate paragraph:

> The conference declares its profound conviction that it would be greatly in the interests of European peace and prosperity if the German people decides for the social-democratic policy of putting the basic industries of the Ruhr under public ownership and socialist control. Under no circumstances must these industries be allowed to return to the private capitalists of any nation.

Outraged by the Adenauer interview, Schumacher went considerably further in his interviews than the Parliamentary Party had envisaged and committed the SPD to intransigent opposition to West German entry into the Ruhr Authority. He was particularly opposed to Adenauer's call for French capital, at a time when the French, under the aegis of Jean Monnet, were trying to build up a powerful steel industry. French policy, in his eyes, was designed to gain control of German industry, a stratagem that was being aided by Adenauer's habit of premature concessions. West Germany should refuse to enter the Ruhr Authority under the present conditions. West German entry would legitimise foreign interference in the West German economy and would hamper German freedom of action in the future. In specific terms it would hamper nationalisation: 'What is being negotiated today is not a matter of today, but of tomorrow and the day after.'[26] Schumacher attempted to have a foreign policy debate in the Bundestag while the Conference was going on.

> The policy of making offers is a bad one and we have demanded a foreign policy debate in parliament in order to let the French know what we do not want.[27]

This suggestion was not only turned down by Adenauer but was also opposed by some members of the Parliamentary Party. Schumacher's position on the International Ruhr Authority, already weakened by the attitude of the SFIO was seriously threatened by a telegram on the IAR from the Labour Party on 13 November, in reply to a memorandum the SPD had sent the Labour Party in August 1949:

> The Executive Committee have come to the unanimous view that a suspension of dismantling was to be welcomed as soon as the Allied governments were convinced that the measures to be taken are sufficient to safeguard their future security. These include the recognition of the Military Security Board and of the Ruhr Authority by the German government.

The results of the Paris Conference were communicated to Adenauer by the High Commissioners at a meeting on the Petersberg on 15 November 1949. Adenauer declared himself in favour of membership of the Military Security Board but expressed reservations concerning Article 31 of the Ruhr Statute, which he felt could be interpreted as meaning that West Germany would, in joining the Ruhr Authority, issue a blank cheque for all the decisions taken by the six countries which had drawn up the Ruhr Statute in 1948 in London. The three High Commissioners were agreed that this was not the case: Article 31 was only concerned to stress the binding nature of majority decisions. Adenauer then declared himself in agreement with West German entry provided that this interpretation was confirmed by the Benelux countries.[29]

26

This assurance was communicated by Adenauer to the Bundestag in the first foreign policy debate, held that same afternoon. [30] Schumacher in his reply concentrated his attention on the style of Adenauer's foreign policy, particularly his neglect of parliament.

> A federal government which does not possess the democratic legitimation of a standpoint which has been discussed in parliament is in a very weak position to withstand foreign pressures. [31]

There was some justification for this standpoint as can be seen in Adenauer's *Memoirs*.

> It must be remembered that the Bundestag was a very young parliament and many of its members were apt to try meddling in the executive where they had no business. . . . The SPD tried to exert a decisive influence on foreign policy by way of the Foreign Affairs Committee, whose Chairman was a Social Democrat, Carlo Schmid. [32]

In contrast to his usual view, Schumacher maintained that moves towards West European integration should be supported even if Great Britain and the Scandinavian countries felt unable to participate. This tradition of a unified Europe, however, was a tradition of freedom and understanding between peoples, not a tradition of understanding between heavy industry interests. In this speech, he attacked for the first time the idea of what he called a 'Junktim', the granting of a concession by the Western Allies in return for a new West German undertaking. In this case it involved making a halt to the dismantling, conditional on West German entry into the International Ruhr Authority. He also objected very strongly to Article 15 of the Ruhr Statute which seemed to make the IAR legally sovereign in a restricted field. Article 19, which spoke of IAR control of the coal, coke and steel industry, seemed to him to require that the Allied governments give various guarantees to the Federal government. Schumacher attacked foreign control of the Ruhr industries, which he thought could only exacerbate an already dangerous social situation. This situation would be alleviated if the trade unions were involved in running the IAR. He also made the point that the IAR would make nationalisation more difficult. Schumacher concluded this speech with a very clear exposition of what he considered to be the rationale of SPD policy. [33]

> The Social Democratic Party sees in the preservation of the interests of the nation the best guarantee that the interests of other nations will be respected and it believes that people can only be involved in

international co-operation through moral, political and social self-assertion.[34]

Carlo Schmid, closing for the opposition, attacked the logic of Adenauer's policy of acceptance of the status quo in the hope of changing it, and emphasised that West Germany must not sign treaties hoping that they would be revised in the future. If the government disagreed with the provisions of a treaty, they should refuse to sign.[35] After this debate, on 17 November, Adenauer again met the High Commissioners on the Petersberg. Not surprisingly, he felt that his position had been weakened by Carlo Schmid's remarks about signing with mental reservations.[36] He was reassured by the High Commissioners on Article 31. The number of plants to be struck from the dismantling list was raised from six to twelve. Adenauer, in order to square his position with his earlier opposition, asked for a passage in the communiqué regarding the new Petersberg agreement to the effect that the Federal government considered some provisions of the Ruhr Agreement to have been rendered obsolete by later developments, and that the Federal government, desiring a review of the agreement, wished to participate in the negotiations on it.[37] In the days between this meeting and the publication of the Petersberg Protocol on 24 November, the SPD were informed, though not consulted, about the contents of the agreement. There were complaints about Adenauer's growing authoritarianism in the SPD Parliamentary Party meeting on 23 November.[38]

The preamble to the protocol stated that its primary aim was to bring about German membership of the European Community. The protocol also expressed a desire that Germany become an associate member of the Council of Europe and sign a bilateral treaty with the USA for receipt of Marshall Aid. The West German government was to request admission to the IAR, to ensure that West Germany remain demilitarised, and it was to co-operate with the Military Security Board. West Germany was to be allowed to construct ships up to 7,200 tons. A number of factories were to be removed from the dismantling list, including eleven synthetic fuel plants and seventeen steel plants.

In his opening speech in the debate of 24 November, Adenauer explained why he was prepared to accept agreements which appeared to limit West German sovereignty:

> I must emphasise yet again that the method of German foreign policy must be to advance slowly and gradually. It must have a psychological basis and be calculated to win back the trust that we Germans largely lost through the National Socialist regime.[39]

He laid great stress on the fact that no real rights were being given up:

> It is not true to say that we are giving up sovereign rights by sending a member to the IAR. Because, Ladies and Gentlemen, we do not possess these rights; they were taken away from us by the unconditional surrender and by the London Agreement. [40]

The SPD's constitutional expert, Dr Adolf Arndt, challenged Adenauer's view that the Basic Law did not oblige him to obtain parliamentary ratification of West German entry into the Ruhr Authority, and called for a total co-operation of peoples, rather than an alliance of ruling classes. [41] Professor Baade, the second speaker for the SPD, made great play about foreign opposition to dismantling, including that of some Labour members of the British parliament. [42] The identification with the Labour government was a major handicap for the SPD, however, given the dismantling policy of the British government. Baade inveighed against the 'Mentalität des Junktims' and the weakening of the German position by her entry into the Ruhr Authority, quoting from Adenauer's earlier speeches against it. Like Arndt's it was a very weak speech. SPD speakers were uneasily conscious that 'opposition' to West German entry would be interpreted as meaning that they acquiesced in continued dismantling.

Late in the evening of the same day, Adenauer played his trump card: he read a telegram which he had received from the DGB Executive in Düsseldorf, welcoming the signing of the protocol. The telegram stated that although the protocol was not completely satisfactory, the government's decision to accept membership of the IAR had been the right one, especially since the government's fears about Article 31 had proved to be groundless. [43] Adenauer had in fact known quite early in the week that the DGB would support him. [44] There was an immediate acrid dispute between Adenauer and Schumacher as to whether or not it was a telegram or merely an agency report. [45] Fisch of the KPD then attacked Adenauer for his refusal to consult parliament. The DGB telegram did not represent the views of the workers. The Ruhr Statute amounted to annexation. He concluded with a call for a united front of all Germans for unity and independence. [46] Ollenhauer was thus placed in the unenviable position of countering Adenauer's bombshell, while avoiding a too close identification with the KPD. This he attempted by stressing the SPD contribution to the halt in dismantling. The psychological unpreparedness of the SPD leadership for a divergence of views with the DGB was demonstrated by Ollenhauer's claim that there had been no properly constituted Executive meeting of the DGB, only an expression of opinion by individual members of the Executive. He concluded by referring hopefully to the Denkschrift which the DGB had submitted to Adenauer at the beginning of the week. [47] This had demanded workers' representation in the IAR. Adenauer then announced that the authenticity of the telegram from the DGB had been confirmed by telephone from Düsseldorf, which he followed by asking rhetorically if the SPD were prepared to send a representative to the Ruhr Authority or not. If not, it must be assumed, in the light of General Robertson's statements, that they wanted dismantling to continue to the bitter end. [48]

Schumacher by this time was completely beside himself with rage because of what he considered to be the disloyal attitude of the DGB, and the accusation that the SPD's policy was calculated to help dismantling was the last straw. The first resolution the SPD had introduced in parliament had been against dismantling. Conscious that he had been out-manoeuvred on an issue on which he had hoped to capitalise, and unable to control himself any longer, Schumacher branded Adenauer as the 'Chancellor of the Allies' and was promptly suspended. [49]

The Parliamentary Party held an immediate meeting. Schumacher's position was presented by his close colleague, Fritz Henssler, who made three main points: (a) Schumacher's ejaculation must be seen as an answer to Adenauer's provocation; (b) Schumacher was prepared to compromise; (c) Adenauer's remark must be seen as an attack on the whole Parliamentary Party. [50] However, Schumacher's intransigent opposition collapsed fairly quickly and, after apologising, he was allowed back into parliament on 2 December.

Though relations with the DGB, and particularly Böckler, were already badly strained, they were exacerbated by an interview given by Böckler on 12 December, in which he vigorously defended the DGB position on the grounds that it would create more jobs and that some of the German representatives would be trade unionists. [51] The DGB's comment of 7 January 1950 was, however, considerably more critical of the IAR. [52] Ollenhauer used the occasion of the Party Executive meeting in Berlin on 5–6 January, to criticise the DGB for disregarding criticisms of the Ruhr Authority by the Trade Union Economics section under Dr Agartz. [53]

In the dispute over West German entry into the IAR the essential nature of the conflict between Schumacher and Adenauer had been made clear. In essence this conflict can be reduced to the age-old contrast between the fox and the lion. Both were concerned with attaining the maximum sovereignity for the Federal Republic and both considered their policy pragmatic. However, they defined sovereignty and pragmatism differently. The kind of sovereignty Adenauer sought was the abolition of the occupation status and some limited freedom of manoeuvre within a highly integrated Western bloc. This type of sovereignty thus involved giving up its essence, once gained, to contractual agreements that would bind Germany to the West in integrative international structures. This policy demanded for its success the political instincts of a fox, of a Laval, since it involved winning freedom of manoeuvre by acceptance of the status quo as defined by the occupying powers.

Schumacher, in contrast, defined sovereignty in a legalistic manner. In this view, Adenauer's policy of giving away rights, even, as was usually the case, rights that West Germany did not possess, would prevent her ever attaining full legal sovereignty and adversely affect the chances of reunification. Schumacher held Adenauer's policy to be the opposite of pragmatic. What Adenauer was actually doing was closing options for West Germany before he had to by entering into a series of binding commitments. In the case of the Ruhr Authority, the option foreclosed, public ownership of the mines, was a very important part of SPD domestic policy. Schumacher, like de Gaulle, maintained that it is precisely when one is weak that one ought not to enter into binding commitments.

Adenauer's and Schumacher's differing conceptions of sovereignty reflect not only a fundamental difference of tactics but also of purpose. Adenauer's view of sovereignty involved West Germany's playing an important role in the formulation of Western foreign policy. It did not involve preserving domestic policy options for the West German government. Schumacher, in contrast, was attempting to strike a difficult balance. On the one hand he tended to stress a legalistic conception of sovereignty in order to preserve domestic options, while, on the other, being acutely aware of the dangers to German reunification of too great a stress on the sovereignty of West Germany.

Although the dispute over German entry into the IAR foreshadowed the later debates in many respects, there was one important difference in that Schumacher continued to maintain that West German membership of the IAR would not be binding on any future SPD government, since the measure had not received parliamentary ratification. [54]

The Kaisen crisis

By this time Schumacher's opposition to entry into the International Ruhr Authority and, even more, the style of his opposition provoked some dissent in the party, notably from Wilhelm Kaisen, Minister President of Bremen. Kaisen had supported Schumacher's efforts to reorganise the party. He had become a member of the Executive in 1946 and had been re-elected in 1947 and 1948 with convincing majorities. Kaisen was, however, a very committed European. Like Adenauer, he held that the two questions, German re-unification and European integration, must be considered separately. Progress was possible in European integration and its possible harmful long-term effects on the prospect of German re-unification must not be allowed to halt it. [55] He therefore became a member of MSEUE, an organisation whose dominating spirit was André Philip, and which held the view that European unity rather than the creation of socialism was the main goal of present day politics. Kaisen attended the Hague Conference of 1948 as a representative of that organisation, though the SPD, like the Labour Party, did not attend officially.

Kaisen's view that the co-operation with the bourgeois parties that had proved so advantageous to the SPD in Bremen might prove equally effective at a national level also contributed to gradually deteriorating relations between Schumacher and himself. This conflict between Kaisen and Schumacher is first evident in a letter from Kaisen to Schumacher on 19 January 1949, criticising Schumacher's assumption that he could act independently of the party organs, especially the Executive, and indicating Kaisen's support for the IAR. [56]

Relations reached a nadir when, a few days before the Bundestag debate of 24 November, Kaisen spoke in favour of Adenauer and West German entry into the IAR to a group of SPD officials. [57]

Kaisen's next letter, on 26 November 1949, was written to Fritz Heine, as he felt Schumacher would not even bother to read it. He denied the parallel maintained by Schumacher between the situation after 1918 and after 1945. The danger of right-wing nationalism had to a large extent been neutralised, since it was a right-wing government that had signed the Ruhr Statute. The SPD would put this in jeopardy if they pursued a nationalist line. He particularly regretted Schumacher's remark about 'Chancellor of the Allies' and asked that it be discussed at the next Executive meeting. [58] He continued to reiterate his objections in two further letters of 8 and 11 December 1949. [59] When Schumacher failed to reply to these letters, and the editor of *Neuer Vorwärts* refused to publish his criticism, Kaisen took the unusual step of criticising Schumacher in an article in the Dutch socialist newspaper *Het Paarool* of Amsterdam on 23 December 1949. [60]

Reaction to this step followed quickly. Fritz Heine announced on 24 December that the Party Executive, which was to meet in Berlin on 5 and 6 January 1950, would discuss Kaisen's statement. [61] At his meeting Kaisen defended the arguments he had advanced in the article, but maintained that it was only a preliminary draft which had been printed without his permission. He had only agreed to let the draft leave his possession to help in writing up the interview that the *Het Paarool* reporter had had with him.

However, Kaisen was completely isolated on the Executive. Even Ernst Reuter, his only powerful ally against Schumacher, voted against him, on the grounds that the freedom of intra-party debate did not justify such an attack on the Party Chairman. [62]

Kaisen defended himself again before the SPD Parliamentary Party on 9 January 1950. His speech was very largely a résumé of his article in *Het Paarool*. It condemned especially Schumacher's charge that Adenauer was betraying the national interest, and stressed the dependence of West Germany on Marshall Aid. He advocated whole-hearted participation in West European political and economic co-operation. He received almost no votes in support of this line. [63] Finally Kaisen explained his position to the local Bremen SPD at the end of January. [64] While there was great personal sympathy for Kaisen expressed at this meeting, there was very little political support.

Kaisen had now been decisively defeated in the Executive, in the Parliamentary Party and at the local level, and after this period, though he continued to pursue an independent line, he made no further effort to challenge Schumacher directly and delegates were instructed to vote him off the Party Executive at the Hamburg Conference in May. [65] This was a clear example of Schumacher's vindictiveness and over-reaction to intra-party opponents, since Kaisen no longer represented any real threat.

The SPD and the Council of Europe

Introduction

The conflict joined on the issue of West German participation in the International Ruhr Authority deepened with the SPD opposition to West German entry into the Council of Europe.

The Council of Europe had grown out of the Hague Conference of the European Movement in 1948, which had demanded the creation of a European consultative assembly. A memorandum to this effect was delivered to the interested governments on 18 August 1948. The French and Belgian governments were favourably disposed towards the idea and agreed to submit the memorandum to the Permanent Commission of the Western European Union (the Brussels Treaty Powers). This draft was opposed by the British government, and the statute of the Council of

Europe published on 5 May 1949 represented an uneasy compromise between British and French conceptions. Two principal organs were created, a Council of Ministers and a Consultative Assembly, but the latter was only empowered to recommend certain courses of action to the Council of Ministers and had no real way of exerting any appreciable pressure on member governments.

SPD opposition to the Council of Europe

The SPD opposition to West German membership of the Council of Europe was essentially based on two issues, that of equality and the question of the Saar. In line with the position he had taken on the International Ruhr Authority, Adenauer was prepared to accept membership with restrictions, meaning associate membership. Schumacher, ever mindful of his success in extracting concessions from the Allies in the constitutional crisis that preceded the establishment of the Federal Republic, insisted on full membership for West Germany. Adenauer's belief in integration and close identification with France meant that he accepted, albeit reluctantly, the simultaneous entry of West Germany and the Saar into the Council of Europe. Schumacher regarded this as a disastrous policy, since it involved, in his view, the legitimation by a West German government of the separation of the Saar from Germany. In the view of the SPD this would seriously prejudice West Germany's position on the 'lost territories'. It was not that the SPD believed that unification was imminent at this time, but more a question of not closing options. A parallel can be drawn with the attitudes of the SPD leadership on domestic policy. They would have agreed that many of their goals looked unattainable in the prevailing conditions, but would nevertheless have defended their retention. Such an attitude in relation to domestic policy lost the SPD many votes; in relation to foreign policy it mainly lost them foreign support.

The first statement by a member of the SPD on the Council of Europe came in a speech by Carlo Schmid on 13 June 1949, to the German section of the European Movement in Wiesbaden. [66] Schmid gave the new institution a guarded welcome in this speech. He was in favour of a unified European political system but felt that the Council of Europe as set out in the statute of 5 May, fell far short of this ideal. What was wanted was a European federation with responsibility for foreign affairs, defence, some financial matters and traffic, and based on a directly elected parliament. This Europe ought not to be directed against anyone, or else it would break up when the threat passed, and ought not to be concerned with defending narrow class interests. It should not be a little Europe, but

34

ought to embrace the whole of continental Europe. From this standpoint the statute's weaknesses were obvious. It was firmly international rather than supranational. It represented only a small part of Europe. Power rested entirely with the Council of Ministers, who would be rendered impotent by the operation of the unanimity rule. Despite its limitations, however, he still regarded it as an advance, though he had reservations about West German entry, thinking it would perhaps deepen the division of Germany. [67]

In contrast to Schmid's guarded welcome, the first official SPD statement on the Council of Europe, made by the Foreign Policy Committee of the party, meeting in Cologne on 5 September 1949, held that 'the admission of the Saar as a member of the Council of Europe would make West German entrance impossible'. [68]

Kurt Schumacher, in the first foreign policy debate on 21 September 1949, rejected Adenauer's policy of accepting the simultaneous entrance of the Saar into the Council of Europe. Such a policy, in Schumacher's view, would only create a *fait accompli* which would be impossible to reverse. If the claim to the Saar were given up it would encourage the hegemonial tendencies that the 'Europeans' claimed they were attempting to overcome, and would weaken the desire of the broad masses of the German people for international co-operation. Such a step would compromise the German position on the Oder–Neisse line, since it would involve the acceptance of a solution prior to the signing of the peace treaty. [69] These points were again repeated by Schumacher at his November press conference and in the debate of 15 November 1949. [70]

Speaking at the close of the same debate, Carlo Schmid, while condemning 'little Europe', came to exactly the opposite conclusion.

> We should only attempt to go to Strasbourg as an associate member since we will only be invited at that level. I believe that if we restrict ourselves to the possible more will be gained than by pursuing a fictive equality. [71]

In the following months the SPD opposition to entry into the Council of Europe was concentrated on the Saar question. The Saar territory had been separated from Germany as early as 17 January 1946, when Bidault announced that the Saar mines were to become French property and that the Saar territory was to become part of the French customs and monetary system. The American and the British governments expressed their approval of the separation of the Saar from Germany and reiterated their support at the Moscow Conference of April 1947. The Saar territory had been detached from the economic control of the zonal government on

22 December 1946, at which time the French customs boundary was extended to the Saar's eastern border. A constitutional Commission created on 23 May 1947 drafted a constitution, the preamble to which stated that the Saar was to be politically independent of Germany and linked in a monetary and customs union with France, which would be responsible for the Saar's defence and foreign relations. The constitution was approved by the Landtag on 8 November 1947, and was officially proclaimed on 15 December 1947. By 1949, however, discontent was growing in the Saar. The French government decided to negotiate a series of conventions with the Saar government, hoping thus to defend its economic advantages, assuage the Saar leaders and impress the West German government with the irrevocable nature of the Saar's French ties.

The SPD position had always been one of militant hostility to the establishment of an independent Saar. The party's first important resolution on the subject, passed at the Bremen meeting of the Party Executive on 13–14 November 1947, insisted that the Saar was German, though it was prepared to recognise French economic interests in the area. After the establishment of the Federal Republic, the party continued its intransigent stance. Resolution 13 of the Bad Dürkheim Resolutions of 29–30 August, confirmed at the small party conference of 5–6 September 1949 in Cologne, insisted that the Saar remain part of Germany. Schumacher repeated his objections at his November press conferences and on 8 January 1950, at the conference of the Berlin SPD. [72]

Some negotiations on the Franco-Saar conventions had taken place between the French and the Saar governments before French Foreign Minister Schuman's visit to Bonn on 13–14 January. Adenauer was, however, unable to exert pressure on Schuman concerning the Saar issue, since Schuman implied that if he were to give way to Germany on the Saar he would be replaced by Bidault, who took a much stronger line on the French presence there. In a conference between Schuman and Schumacher on 14 January, Schumacher used virtually the same arguments as Adenauer. [73] Ollenhauer, in fact, explicitly stated that Adenauer's views on the Saar were in essence identical to those of the SPD. [74] Schumacher, however, in his press conference of 16 January, went much further than Adenauer would have been prepared to go, saying that the best protest against the projected Franco–Saar agreements would be a West German refusal to join the Council of Europe. [75] Schuman refused Adenauer's request for a conference on the Saar issue and it proved impossible to issue a joint communiqué. While Schuman's final press conference was conciliatory, Adenauer's arguments at his own press conference embraced many aspects of Schumacher's position. [76] Despite German protests, the

36

Franco–Saar negotiations took place in Paris between 7 February and 3 March 1950. [77]

As soon as the text of the agreed conventions was published, Dr Adenauer said that he did not now expect a majority for West German entry into the Council of Europe nor would he request it. He expected all parties to oppose the agreements, which would complicate European discussions incalculably and might even render them hopeless for some time to come. [78] At a press conference on 4 March, he said that the conventions were a 'decision against Europe', and a breach of the Potsdam Agreement motivated exclusively by 'French hunger for gold'. He asked M. Schuman to let the Saar problem rest until Germany was a member of the Council of Europe, an entry which had now been jeopardised by his refusal to do so. [79] Adenauer condemned these conventions in an interview on 7 March with the American correspondent, Kingsbury-Smith, but proposed a Franco–German Union, of which the return of the Saar was a precondition. [80] On 7 March 1950 the SPD Executive issued a memorandum on the Saar. This opposed the Saar's admission to the Council of Europe on the grounds that this would amount to a recognition of the Saar's sovereignty, and that a united Europe ought not to begin with an undemocratic act. The promise in the convention to reconsider the situation at a final peace conference was an empty formula, since the conference might never be held. It concluded that a solution must be found which would take account of legitimate French interests, but which would not mean ratification of a French annexation. [81]

In the Parliamentary Party meeting of 9 March 1950, Hermann Brill requested that entry into the Council of Europe should not be coupled with the Saar question. He was opposed by Schumacher who, however, conceded that the SPD would have to be prepared to send representatives to the Council if it was outvoted. [82]

In the special Bundestag debate on the conventions on 10 March 1950, Schumacher made a very intransigent speech rejecting the conventions. He reminded the Bundestag that, according to the conventions, the Saar was to be represented abroad by France. This of itself ought to debar the entry of the Saar into the Council of Europe. The Saar must be allowed to choose between France and Germany. [83]

The SPD memorandum on the Saar mentioned above was the basis of the SPD case in a debate about the Saar on 18–19 March in Hastings. The SPD, represented at the conference by Erich Ollenhauer, Gerhart Luetkens and Erwin Grath, was the only party to reject the conventions of 3 March. [84] They were similarly isolated at the Copenhagen meeting of Comisco at the beginning of June. [85]

The Hamburg Conference and after

The Hamburg Conference of 21–25 May 1950, was the most important Party Conference since the war. It provided the first chance for the party as a whole to consider the Schumacher style of 'opposition' since the establishment of the Federal Republic. The key speech was made by Schumacher.[86] Nearly all the arguments he had used against Adenauer's foreign policy in the preceding months reappeared in this speech. Schumacher's characteristic emphasis on legal sovereignty led him to ask for the repeal of the Occupation Statute. In this connection he pointed out a logical contradiction in Allied policy, in that they simultaneously invited West Germany to join the Council of Europe because it was a democratic country, yet maintained at the London Conference that the removal of the Occupation Statute depended on the realisation of democracy in West Germany. He rejected the identification of Europe with the area covered by Charlemagne's Empire. In his view the interest in European unity and internationalism displayed by the CDU only masked sinister class interests.

> An international vocabulary does not necessarily create an international reality and the internationalism of a class interest does not imply the internationalism of peoples.

Although he repeated his earlier objections to the coupling of the entry of the Saar and West Germany into the Council of Europe, he framed his objections in very broad terms.

> Europe can only be built on the basis of European solidarity and the European friendship of free and equal peoples. It can fulfill its function against the totalitarian claims from the East only with the maximum of democratic strength not as part of a victor–vanquished construction.

Moreover, Adenauer's claim that signing agreements and assenting to the Saar Convention would not affect the final peace treaty was misconceived, since Adenauer's actions rendered a final peace treaty very doubtful. If a final peace conference were in fact held, German freedom of manoeuvre would be very small precisely because Adenauer had contracted a whole series of binding agreements.

Although the Party Conference took place before the question of West German rearmament had really begun to be debated, Schumacher was already worried about the possible implications of West German membership of the Council of Europe or, later, on entry into NATO. The

Council of Europe in his view was important only as a portal to NATO. If West Germany were to enter the Council of Europe under the present conditions, she would find it impossible to refuse entry to NATO under the same conditions, and this would leave her powerless to alter or influence the 'scorched earth' policy of NATO.

Schumacher concluded by criticising Adenauer for his failure to consult or inform the opposition. In his final peroration against West German entry, he claimed that this, under the unfavourable conditions suggested, would encourage German nationalism. A further and even more serious danger was that the Europe that was being created would, because of its undemocratic and anti-socialist nature, be very vulnerable to communist pressure.

Opposition to Schumacher crystallised around the Länder politicians. Wilhelm Kaisen, defeated in January, had decided not to attend and was in the United States, but Max Brauer led the attack on Schumacher. Brauer drew a parallel with Weimar experience and cited Karl Kautsky, who had written in favour of German entry into the League of Nations before Germany had been invited to join. While sharing Schumacher's views on the Saar, he held that the present situation could best be altered by joining the Council. [87] Brauer was followed immediately by Paul Löbe, who felt that Schumacher should make his criticism in Strasbourg rather than Hamburg. The United States of Europe was such an important goal that disadvantages and difficulties must be ignored. [88] Ernst Reuter had sent Willy Brandt to speak on his behalf. While Brandt professed to agree with two-thirds of what Schumacher had said, he still supported West German entry. [89] Otto Bach, traditionally the most European member of the Berlin SPD, was against entry on the grounds that the Council of Europe did not go far enough towards a united Europe. [90] Heydorn of Hamburg pointed out, in a very pro-European speech, that the party leadership had failed to develop a convincing alternative to the Council of Europe. [91]

Schumacher's policy was supported principally by Eichler, Schmid, Henssler, Lüdemann and Schoettle. [92] Herbert Wehner (Hamburg) introduced a resolution on behalf of the Hamburg Party (Resolution no. 25), calling on the Party Executive to make greater efforts to co-ordinate party policy on important political questions in the Bundesrat, Executive and Parliamentary Party. This resolution was obviously designed to reduce the independent tendencies of the 'Bürgermeisterflügel'. [93]

Schumacher concluded the debate by pointing to his success in the constitutional crisis and asserting the necessity for equality in international affairs. The SPD would vote against entry into the Council of Europe because of the reunification problem. However, he welcomed the idea of the Schuman Plan, though he stressed that it was only a suggestion. In general his speech was very nationalistic in tone. [94]

The Conference was a complete victory for Schumacher. The Executive's resolution was almost unanimously adopted — eleven delegates voted against it and four abstained. The resolution approved the standpoint of the Executive and the Parliamentary Party on the issue of entry into the Council of Europe. It deplored the simultaneous entrance of the Saar and the Federal Republic into the Council of Europe. The current misuse of European idealism would give Eastern totalitarianism a chance. In rejecting the IAR and German entry into the Council of Europe, the SPD had demonstrated its desire to work for a united Europe. The Schuman Plan was welcome as a political step which should not be influenced by experts who only represented class interests. The final position of the SPD would depend on the specific contents of the Schuman Plan. [95] Schumacher had sent instructions to the various districts not to vote for Kaisen and he was duly voted off the Executive. Reuter remained on the Executive but dropped to sixteenth on the list.

Resolution 60, which had been substituted for Wehner's Resolution no. 25, but which expressed identical sentiments, was adopted by an overwhelming majority. [96] The Länder politicians had been resoundingly defeated and Schumacher's support in the party convincingly demonstrated. [97]

The Hamburg Conference had its effects on the Bundesrat debate on West German entry on 25 May 1950. This was the first parliamentary debate on the question of West German entry and Adenauer considered the occasion important enough to request permission to speak.

The Conference debate in Hamburg and the passing of Resolution no. 60, had effected Hamburg's position. Paul Nevermann, who spoke for the Hamburg delegation, admitted that the desire to take part in international institutions was strong in Hamburg, but argued that the arguments against entry on national grounds, namely the lack of German equality and the coupling of German entry with that of the Saar were overwhelming. [98] This position was also taken by Stock of Hesse. [99] Adenauer, who concluded the debate, hardly mentioned the Council of Europe. [100] Entry was justified and likely to lead to German participation in the Schuman Plan. The final vote went as expected. Bremen voted for the government despite Kaisen's continued absence in the United States. Hamburg, Lower Saxony, Schleswig-Holstein and Hesse all voted against.

The Comiso Conference held in Copenhagen on 1–5 June, managed to produce an agreed communiqué on the Saar. [101]

The Bundestag debate on German entry, which had been planned for 6 June, but postponed because of Adenauer's illness, actually took place on 13 June. Adenauer spoke first for the government. The bulk of his speech dealt with the Schuman Plan. Aware of disquiet, particularly in the FDP, about the Saar Conventions, Adenauer concentrated on defending the simultaneous entry of the Saar. He laid great stress on the assurance by the Allied High Commissioners that the Saar Conventions would not prejudge the outcome of the final peace treaty negotiations. Adenauer was, moreover, able to point out that the SPD, by participating in Comisco Conferences with Saar SPS representatives, had severely compromised its position of non-recognition of an independent Saar. [102]

Kurt Schumacher's speech was little more than a repeat performance of his opening address at the Hamburg Party Conference. Once again, the Saar was treated as an issue of principle. If the principle of self-determination was discounted in the West, it would be impossible to prevent its being discounted in the East. Such a situation was bound, in Schumacher's view, to create a nationalist backlash in West Germany. In attacking Adenauer's defence of the Saar Conventions, Schumacher gave a particularly clear indication of the long term strategic considerations behind his opposition to Adenauer's foreign policy.

> The peace treaty which will eventually appear will not be a sudden revolutionary legal act in favour of the Germans, but will rather be made up of a mosaic of *faits accomplis* against which the Germans have put up too little resistance. [103]

The weakest part of Schumacher's argumentation was his attempt to reject an assertion of Adenauer's that those who voted against entry were against the West. Given the profound public sympathy for the idea of European unity, this was Adenauer's strongest card, and Schumacher's claim that rejection of entry would save the West Germans from disillusionment looked very thin indeed. Voting took place on 15 June 1950. The SPD and KPD were the only parties to vote against entry, the result of the voting being 218 votes for the government to 151 against, with 9 abstentions.

It had seemed as if Hermann Brill, the Parliamentary Party's most committed European, would abstain. In a letter of 12 June, Brill had made references to the 'Royal Prussian Social Democratic Party' and Schumacher's minimal knowledge of SPD history. He had concluded by indicating that he would abstain.

I find it impossible to support the attempts of the KPD to destroy Europe by voting with them against entry. It is therefore for me a question of conscience not to appear in an anti-European voting bloc with the communist deputies. [104]

In the event however he voted with the SPD.

After the adoption of the Bill, the party continued to criticise the Council of Europe. It was asserted that the Council agreed neither with the SPD's wish to prevent an international union of heavy industry at the expense of the workers, nor to its suggestions on the field to be included in a European federation or to its position on the Saar and German unity. [105]

Nevertheless, when the Party Executive met on 24 June, Schumacher suggested sending delegates to Strasbourg. He was violently opposed by Waldemar von Knoeringen on the grounds that it would damage the party's image after it had so violently opposed German entry into the Council of Europe. Schumacher replied that one could try and prevent a train leaving the station, but if this failed there was nothing left but to jump on as best one could. [106] It was resolved unanimously to send delegates only from the Bundestag. A request from the Bundesrat was turned down as this would have meant including people like Kaisen and Brauer, people who in Schumacher's eyes would undermine the SPD position in Strasbourg. The reversal of policy was justified on the grounds that, as a democratic party, the SPD acquiesced in the will of the majority and that it was therefore incumbent on them to go to Strasbourg to try and influence policy and foster contact with other European socialists. [107]

The Parliamentary Party met on 28 June 1950. Schumacher made three main points: delegates must be chosen only by members of the Parliamentary Party; members of the Bundesrat should not be included; Party unity was necessary in foreign policy.

Baur and Marx both spoke against SPD participation, on the grounds that the Council of Europe was only a bloc for industrial interests, and that for the SPD to send delegates now would damage the Party's credit. All the other speeches supported Schumacher's position. [108]

It was decided to send delegates to Strasbourg while the principle was simultaneously upheld that West Germany should not have accepted the invitation to enter the Council of Europe. This decision was justified on grounds advanced by Luetkens: that Germany could not be represented by Adenauer's supporters alone. The decision not to send Bundesrat members was upheld. [109]

Conclusion

The result of the first Federal election in 1949 had implied a rejection of the SPD's critique of the Christian Democratic social market economy. In the Bundestag Schumacher pursued his notion of 'opposition' in the field of foreign affairs and defence. [110] This had led him to oppose the entry of West Germany into both the International Ruhr Authority and the Council of Europe. In this opposition he had been concerned above all to avoid endorsing agreements which would tend to legitimise the status quo − a weak and divided Germany. The contest joined over the International Ruhr Authority and continued in the debate over West German entry into the Council of Europe seemed to many to be merely the old Weimar one of Erfüllungspolitik (a policy of concessions) *v.* Wiederstandpolitik (a policy of resistance). Schumacher, with his talk of a 'policy of intransigence' did appear at times to be carrying on an 'opposition of principle'. This intransigence has been attributed largely to his physical condition. He suffered from an acute circulatory disease and had one leg and one arm amputated. He was also very conscious of the fact that he would not have very long to live. Lastly, his period in a concentration camp, had bred in him a conviction that he was the only person morally, as well as intellectually, qualified to lead Germany. These factors gave his policies and, even more strikingly, his personality, a certain harshness and intensity which alienated many who would otherwise have supported him, particularly foreign socialists.

In reality, Schumacher's opposition at this time had something of a rhetorical symbolic quality. There was never any danger that the SPD would not accept majority decisions of the Bundestag or carry on extra-parliamentary opposition, and when he skirted the bounds of unconstitutionality with his 'Bundeskanzler der Alliierten' (Chancellor of the Allies) speech on 24 November 1949, he very quickly apologised and little more was heard of a 'policy of intransigence'. There is little doubt, however, that his initial addiction to rhetorical intransigence did the party some damage. The problem was that his whole strategy was focussed on parliamentary action. This meant that when the SPD had been outvoted he had no alternative but to accept the verdict of parliament. This led to great difficulties in the post-war German situation, where people were unused to the rules of the game of parliamentary democracy. It is striking in this connection that the most intense debate in the SPD Parliamentary Party was over the question of sending representatives to the Council of Europe after having opposed it so bitterly.

Moreover, although Schumacher laid great stress on preserving the reunification option, the virulence of his anti-communism meant that his loyalty, and the loyalty of the SPD, to the West and West Germany was never really in doubt. In the last analysis he would always prefer a separate democratic West Germany to a re-unified communist Germany. This identification with the West, combined with a desire to preserve the national option, had tended to blur the edges of his opposition and resulted in the SPD's being distrusted by those both to the right and left of it. It was thus unable to fulfil Schumacher's claim to oppose government policy with 'concrete alternatives tuned to concrete situations'.

Notes

1 See Schumacher's speeches filed under Q10 (1949 speeches) in the library of the Party Executive. This library has been incorporated since 1969 in the Archiv der Sozialendemokratie but I think it is useful for me to give the former notation as this would enable the Archiv to identify the present location of any of the old material.
2 Interviews of A.M. Renger, November 1966, and Arno Scholz, Summer 1967.
3 Konrad Adenauer, *Memoirs*, vol. 1, London 1966, p. 170.
4 L. Edinger, op. cit., p. 206.
5 T. Pirker, op. cit., p. 110.
6 K. Adenauer, op. cit., vol. 1, pp. 177–81.
7 A.J. Heidenheimer, *Adenauer and the CDU. The Rise of the Leader and the Integration of the Party*, The Hague 1960, p. 174–5.
8 *Frankfurter Allgemeine Zeitung (FAZ)*, 15 August 1949.
9 *FAZ*, 15 August 1949. Despite the opposition of both Schumacher and Adenauer, the Länder Minister Presidents of both parties remained in favour of coalition: see their declaration at Koblenz, *Die Welt*, 26 August 1949.
10 *FAZ*, 31 August 1949.
11 T. Pirker, op. cit., p. 126.
12 *FAZ*, 31 August 1949.
13 *Die Welt*, 7 September 1949.
14 This episode is well summarised in T. Pirker, op. cit., p. 116.
15 Deutscher Bundestag, *Verhandlungen*, 20 September 1949 p. 22–30 (K. Adenauer).
16 Ibid., p. 32 (K. Schumacher).
17 Ibid., p. 42 (K. Schumacher). For Schumacher's views on the necessity of equality in international co-operation, see Chapter 1, *passim*.

44

[18] Communiqué issued by the London Six Power Conference, 7 June 1948; *The Times*, London, 8 June 1948.

[19] K. Adenauer, op. cit., vol. 1, pp. 114–5.

[20] Ibid., pp. 196–7.

[21] Ibid., pp. 196–7.

[22] *FAZ*, 8 November 1949. K. Adenauer, op. cit., vol. 1, p. 202.

[23] Cf. Q8 (Press Interviews 1946–52) in Party Library. See also K. Adenauer, op. cit., vol. 1, pp. 203–5.

[24] *Protokoll der Fraktionssitzung*, 22 September. I had privileged access to the *Protokoll* of the Fraktionssitzungen up until Schumacher's death. None of this material has been made available before. I was refused access to the minutes of the Executive, which I understand exist for this period only in a fairly sketchy form.

[25] Ibid.

[26] Press Conference, 12 November 1949 (Q8), cited F.R. Alleman, *Bonn ist nicht Weimar*, Cologne 1956, p. 145.

[27] Press Conference, 12 November 1949 (Q8).

[28] *Protokoll der Fraktionssitzung*, 10 November 1949.

[29] K. Adenauer, op. cit., vol. 1, pp. 208–12.

[30] Deutscher Bundestag, *Verhandlungen*, 15 November 1949, pp. 392–400 (K. Adenauer).

[31] Ibid., p. 401 (K. Schumacher).

[32] K. Adenauer, op. cit., vol. 1, p. 222.

[33] Deutscher Bundestag, *Verhandlungen*, 15 November 1949, pp. 400–8 (K. Schumacher).

[34] Ibid., p. 407.

[35] Ibid., p. 440 (C. Schmid).

[36] K. Adenauer, op. cit., vol. 1, p. 214.

[37] Ibid., p. 220.

[38] *Protokoll der Fraktionssitzung*, 23 November 1949.

[39] Deutscher Bundestag, *Verhandlungen*, 24 November 1949, p. 472 (K. Adenauer).

[40] Ibid., p. 474 (K. Adenauer).

[41] Ibid., pp. 477–8 (A. Arndt).

[42] Ibid., pp. 485–90 (F. Baade).

[43] K. Adenauer, op. cit., vol. 1, pp. 223–5.

[44] See letter from Böckler to Adenauer, 21 November 1949, which I discovered in the DGB Archive.

[45] T. Pirker, op. cit., p. 121.

[46] Deutscher Bundestag, *Verhandlungen*, 24 November 1949, pp. 506–11 (Fisch).

[47] Ibid., pp. 522–4 (E. Ollenhauer).

[48] Ibid., pp. 524–5 (K. Adenauer).

[49] T. Pirker, op. cit., p. 124.

[50] *Protokoll der Fraktionssitzung*, 24 November 1949.

[51] *Kölnische Rundschau*, 13 December 1949.

[52] *FAZ*, 8 January 1950.

[53] *Die Neue Zeitung*, 7 January 1950.

[54] Q11 (Schumacher speeches), 1950.

[55] Kaisen, op. cit., p. 381.

[56] Letter, Kaisen – Schumacher, 19 January 1949, in Kaisen personal archive. I spent a period with Kaisen and he made his personal papers available to me.

[57] Cited in K. Adenauer, op. cit., vol. 1, p. 214.

[58] Letter, Kaisen – Heine, 26 November 1949, in Kaisen personal archive.

[59] Kaisen personal archive.

[60] Copy of *Het Paarool* article, Kaisen personal archive.

[61] *FAZ*, 26 December 1949.

[62] Interview with Kaisen, November 1966, confirmed by interview with A.M. Renger, December 1966, Willi Eichler, August 1967. I have also seen notes on the meeting in Kaisen's personal archive.

[63] *Protokoll der Fraktionssitzung*, 9 January 1950.

[64] *Neuer Vorwärts*, 4/1950.

[65] Interview with Kaisen, confirmed by interview with Eichler and Schoettle, Summer 1967. See also letter from Erich Rossmann, a prominent member of the Stuttgart SPD to Kaisen, 26 May 1950, Kaisen personal archive, where he informs Kaisen that he has been removed from the Party Executive, 'Dank von Herrn Hannover'. He also speaks of Schumacher's totalitarian methods. Ironically Rossman had been instrumental in fostering Schumacher's early career in the Weimar SPD.

[66] C. Schmid, *Deutschland und der Europäische Rat*, Wiesbaden 1949.

[67] Ibid, p. 18.

[68] *Die Welt*, 6 September 1949.

[69] Deutscher Bundestag, *Verhandlungen*, 21 September 1949, p. 42 (K. Schumacher).

[70] *Die Welt*, 16 November 1949.

[71] Deutscher Bundestag, *Verhandlungen*, 29 September 1949, p. 185 (C. Schmid).

[72] Filed under Q8 (press statements 1948–52) and Q11, (speeches 1950).

[73] *Die Neue Zeitung*, 15 January 1949.

[74] *Die Neue Zeitung*, 15 January 1949.

[75] *Die Neue Zeitung*, 18 January 1949. Cf. *Sopade* no. 894, pp. 11–13 for all SPD speeches on the Saar, January 1950.

[76] *Die Neue Zeitung*, 17 January 1949.

[77] See *L'Année Politique*, 1950, p. 355.

[78] *Die Welt*, 4 March 1950.

[79] *Die Welt*, 5 March 1950.

[80] K. Adenauer, op. cit., vol. 1, pp. 244–5.

[81] *Die Sozialdemokratie und das Saarproblem*, Hannover 1950, pp. 19–42.

[82] *Protokoll der Fraktionssitzung*, 9 March 1950.

[83] Deutscher Bundestag, *Verhandlungen*, 10 March 1950, pp. 1562–70 (K. Schumacher).

[84] See *Sopade*, April 1950; also *The Times*, 20 March 1950.

[85] See *Sopade*, July 1950.

[86] 'Die Sozialdemokratie im Kampf um Deutschland und Europa', *Protokoll des Hamburger Parteitages der SPD*, 1950, pp. 62–84. Notes 87–96 also drawn on this source.

[87] *Protokoll*, op. cit., pp. 100–2 (M. Brauer).

[88] *Protokoll*, op. cit., pp. 102–3 (P. Löbe).

[89] *Protokoll*, op. cit., pp. 103–5 (W. Brandt).

[90] *Protokoll*, op. cit., pp. 115–17 (O. Bach).

[91] *Protokoll*, op. cit., pp. 105–7 (H. Heydorn).

[92] *Protokoll*, op. cit., pp. 108–10 (W. Eichler).
Protokoll, op. cit., pp. 110–12 (H. Lüdemann).
Protokoll, op. cit., pp. 112–14 (C. Schmid).
Protokoll, op. cit., pp. 117–19 (E. Schoettle).
Protokoll, op. cit., pp. 144–6 (F. Henssler).

[93] *Protokoll*, op. cit., pp. 121–4 (H. Wehner).

[94] *Protokoll*, op. cit., pp. 156–66.

[95] *Protokoll*, op. cit., p. 274.

[96] *Protokoll*, op. cit., p. 167.

[97] Though Brauer and Kaisen continued to speak in favour of the Council of Europe, see Brauer's speech in Frankfurt, 17 July 1950, *FAZ* 18 July 1950.

[98] Deutscher Bundesrat, *Verhandlungen*, 25 May 1950, pp. 357–8 (K. Adenauer).

[99] Ibid., pp. 358–9 (P. Nevermann). The Hamburg position was decided by the Senate on 23 May. The Bürgerschaft did not discuss the question until 1 June.

[99] Ibid., pp. 361–2 (C. Stock).

[100] Ibid., p. 368.

[101] *The Scotsman*, 6 June 1950.

[102] Deutscher Bundestag, *Verhandlungen*, 13 June 1950, pp. 2459–66 (K. Adenauer).

[103] Ibid., pp. 2470–8 (K. Schumacher). Citation p. 2472.

[104] Letter, Brill – Schumacher, 12 June 1950, (Schumacher correspondence Q21 A-C). This is one of the few letters in the Archive which Schumacher has written on. At three places in the letter he has scribbled 'falsch'. See Chapter 3 for more detail on Brill.

[105] 'Die Aussenpolitik der SPD' pp. 12ff.

[106] Interview, F. Heine, November 1966; W. Eichler, Summer 1967; Waldemar von Knoeringen, September 1969.

[107] *Neuer Vorwärts*, 30 June 1950.

[108] *Protokoll der Fraktionssitzung*, 28 June 1950.

[109] *Neuer Vorwärts*, 30 June 1950.

[110] See W. Kralewski, K.H. Neunreither, *Oppositionelles Verhalten im ersten Deutschen Bundestag, 1949–53*, Cologne 1963.

3   The SPD and
the Schuman Plan

Introduction

On 9 May 1950, Robert Schuman announced to an astonished press conference that the French government proposed 'to place all Franco-German coal and steel production under a common High Authority, in an organisation open to the participation of the other countries of Europe'. This pooling of coal and steel production would 'mean the immediate establishment of common bases of industrial production, which is the first step toward European federation and will change the destiny of regions that have long been devoted to the production of war armaments of which they themselves have been the constant victims'.[1] The *raison d'être* of this policy was rapprochement with Germany. 'Five years, almost to the day, after the Germans' unconditional surrender, France is carrying out the first decisive act in the construction of Europe, in partnership with Germany. The situation in Europe will be completely transformed as a result.'[2] He then laid down a series of rigid conditions upon which the French government would not compromise for the establishment of such a community.

Schuman made his historic statement at a time when the failure of the post-war French policy of keeping Germany weak was becoming obvious. Officially, there were no public proposals for German rearmament but it had been widely mooted in the United States and Britain. A major aim of United States policy in Europe was to keep West Germany tied to the West. West Germany had to be defended for political and military reasons yet at the same time she represented an unused military potential. Clearly events were moving towards increased independence, strength and eventually rearmament for Germany.

These developments posed enormous problems for any French government. Successive French governments had reluctantly acceded to British and American pressure to relax controls on Germany. The International Ruhr Authority, once regarded as a means of continuing Allied control, no longer looked very secure. In the face of these developments the French had few alternatives. 'They could continue backwards along the route they had followed since the end of the war, delaying where they could and hoping something would turn up to divert the course of events and make German revival and the prospect of rearmament less danger- ous.'[3] The weaknesses of such a policy were obvious: too intransigent a resistance to American demands might make the United States feel that they had to choose between France and West Germany. A policy of neutralism was ruled out by all except the Communists. In such a situa- tion France had to develop a new initiative. The pooling of coal and steel, already bruited by Adenauer and Karl Arnold, seemed most likely to find a sympathetic response in West Germany. It would be too simple, how- ever, to see the Schuman Plan simply as a device to counter or contain Germany. Schuman and the Mouvement Républicain Populaire (MRP), in common with most other Christian Democratic parties, had been consis- tently 'European', and the Schuman Plan represented for them a way of achieving a real measure of West European integration — something which had eluded both the Council of Europe and the Organisation for European Economic Co-operation (OEEC).

During 1948 and early 1949, the OEEC had tried to harmonise the national recovery programmes of its members. These attempts had proved to be fruitless, partly because of the complex nature of the problem, but mainly because of the unwillingness of governments to give up their sover- eignty and make drastic adaptations to their plans, which would make them dependent on developments over which they had no control.

Economically there were two main reasons for a Franco—German coal and steel pool, though there is widespread agreement that they were only secondary factors in prompting the French initiative. There was firstly the traditional dependence of the Lorraine steel producing area on coke from the Ruhr. This factor has always constituted France's chief economic interest in a common market for coal and steel. A more immediate factor was the state of steel production in Western Europe. Monsieur Monnet, the chief motivator of the Schuman Plan in his capacity as Director of the Commissariat Général du Plan de Modernisation et d'Équipement, had encouraged the production of steel in France. Crude steel output in 1949 was just over 2 million tons more than in any year since 1929. West Germany's output did not equal France's (excluding the Saar) until 1949. This situation was obviously bound to alter with the falling away of Allied controls. The Economic Commission for Europe concluded, in autumn 1949, that if plans were not modified Europe's steel making capacity in 1953 would be substantially greater than the predictable demand both for consumption and for export.[4]

The Schuman Plan, then, was a product of the interaction of French foreign policy, the revival of Germany, the movement towards European integration and the state of the coal and steel economy of Western Europe. 'The idea of "the pool" provided a solution to problems that had confronted France for several years on the global level, on the European level and on the German level.'[5]

Initial German reaction to Schuman's announcement was predominantly favourable. Adenauer was in fact only informed on the morning of 9 May.[6] In a letter to Adenauer, Schuman wrote that the goal of his plan was political, not economic. It offered an answer to the perennial French fear that a fully recovered Germany would once again attack France. Rearmament was always first noticeable in an increased production of coal, steel and iron. If his plan were carried out, it would be possible to detect the first signs of movement, and this would have a very positive effect on French public opinion.

Adenauer announced his support of the Schuman Plan at a press conference on the evening of the same day, when he also stated that the aim of the West German government was to create a third force in a United Europe, 'a force which would not measure up to the two super-powers, but which would at least have enough political and economic strength to put its weight into the scales for the preservation of peace.' Of the Schuman Plan itself, he said that it was a magnanimous step towards Germany and Europe on the part of France, and stressed that the French proposal was based on the principle of equality. The Schuman Plan also represented a way of solving the Saar problem.[7]

The initial SPD attitude

Schumacher held a press conference on Wednesday, 11 May, to make public the SPD attitude towards the Schuman Plan. As one would expect from the debate over entry into the Council of Europe, his attitude was reserved and cautious. It was still SPD policy at this time to support West European integration. The Council of Europe had been opposed because of insufficient integration. The reunification issue had been raised in the form of the Saar, but the clear implication was that if satisfactory terms could have been got for the Saar, integration should have been pursued. Much more stress had been laid on attaining a position of equality for West Germany than in stressing her provisional status. Schumacher's initial response to the Schuman Plan was purely in terms of the effect it would have on domestic policy options. While he welcomed the plan, the final SPD attitude would depend on the approach taken on nationalisation –

something which was not at all clear from Schuman's press conference. It would also be necessary to settle the co-determination question and to abolish the Ruhr Authority before the plan came into operation. Moreover if the plan were to be anything more than a moderate success, the trade unions would have to be involved.[8]

When he spoke at Neustadt on the following Saturday, 14 May, to the Regional Party Conference of the SPD of the Rhineland Palatinate, his tone was a bit more enthusiastic. This enthusiasm led him to talk in terms of a new era in Europe if the plan were accepted. There were, however, several problems, namely the widely differing steel prices in the two countries and, much more serious for the SPD, given their support of nationalisation, the French government's rejection of the preamble to Law no. 75, by which the decision on the ownership question was to be left to an independent German government. There was also the problem of British membership. On no account must negotiations with Britain fail, since this would lead to a Catholic, conservative, cartellistic Europe separated from the socialist countries of northern Europe. Schumacher's continued suspicion of French policy is apparent in his concluding observation that free entry for French industries must wait until German industries had recovered from the constraining influences of the International Ruhr Authority.[9] In a speech on the following Friday Schumacher said that the Schuman Plan was doubly welcome: firstly, because it was a French initiative, and secondly, because it appeared to be serious.[10]

Schumacher's first really important declaration on the Schuman Plan was made at the Hamburg Party Conference (21–25 May 1950).[11] He welcomed it in his key-note address as the first attempt to get beyond rhetoric and actually accomplish something in the economic field. His fairly sympathetic treatment of the Schuman Plan was in marked contrast to his swingeing attacks on the Council of Europe.

In essence, Schumacher's remarks on the Schuman Plan revolved around the necessity of British participation to act as a counterweight to conservative forces, the importance of preserving the nationalisation option, and the abolition of the Ruhr Authority as a precondition for the establishment of the coal and steel pool. As in the debate over entry into the Council of Europe, great weight was laid on German equality. Schumacher was, however, much more critical of Adenauer's handling of the negotiations than of the plan itself. The Schuman Plan represented, in Schumacher's view, a major political intitiative. This initiative could not succeed without the SPD, since the SPD represented the interests of the Labour movement. (In this case, as with the IAR, Schumacher was unable to comprehend that the DGB leadership might differ from the SPD.) The

Federal government had seriously damaged the initiative by entrusting the negotiation on discussion to experts, who were always the mere tools of capitalist interests, rather than to politicians. Schumacher closed his speech with an attack on the managers — the archetypes of Monnet's Europe — linking this to his anti-communism.

> The super-state of the managers would pave the way for the successful invasion of national-communist ideas from the East. [12]

The question of the Schuman Plan, unlike that of entry into the Council of Europe, provoked little controversy and Resolution 71 was passed without any difficulty.

> On the Schuman Plan the Party Conference declares that it welcomes any attempt that will lead to serious negotiations. It recognises in the suggestion of the French Foreign Minister a political initiative that must not be allowed to be influenced by experts who are really only the tools of special interests. The SPD is convinced that an organisation of Western Europe on the basis of the interests of heavy industry would be a fatal blow to democracy and the prospects of international co-operation between peoples on the basis of equality. The SPD reserves its final position until it knows the content of a series of discussions. Especially important will be the equality of all partners, the position of the Ruhr Authority and the right of the German people to decide about questions of ownership in their economy. [13]

Almost immediately after the Hamburg Conference, a meeting of the Socialist International was held in London on 16–17 June to determine the attitude of the socialist parties of Western Europe towards the Schuman initiative. By this time it was clear that the ailing British Labour government was not going to participate in the Schuman Plan, and the SPD attitude consequently became distinctly cooler. Fierce debate ensued between the British and Scandinavian parties on the one side, and the Dutch socialists on the other, regarding the merits of the supranational principle. The Schuman Declaration was, however, cautiously approved by the Conference in an eleven point declaration. The SPD, however, only agreed to sign this communiqué on the understanding that the Ruhr Authority would be phased out and Germany accorded a position of absolute equality. The communiqué stated that:

> 1 The Schuman Declaration was to be welcomed and it underlined the point that only by planning could economic stability be preserved.

2   The Conference greeted with enthusiasm the stated aim of the Schuman Plan to raise living standards – an aim which must not be allowed to be thwarted by those who would attempt to use the Schuman Plan for restrictive purposes.

3   The Schuman Declaration was as yet only a suggestion and care must be taken to ensure that the final institution was in conformity with points one and two.

4   Working conditions and standards of living in the countries which were a party to the plan must be successively improved to the level of the more progressive countries.

5   The only security that this would be the case was the full participation of the trade unions.

6   The European Coal and Steel Organisation must be efficiently organised.

7   The governments must agree to a co-ordinated investment programme in order to increase demand. New investments were necessary in less developed countries overseas as well as in Europe.

8   Governments taking part in such an organisation must undertake to carry out decisions arrived at jointly.

9   Any harmful effects of the plan must be borne equally by all countries.

10   Any organisation must be established on a democratic basis. This implied trade union and consumer participation in the machinery.

11   The Schuman Plan must be established on the basis of full employment. If all eleven points were observed the plan would represent a real step forward. [14]

Schumacher, although by now cool towards the idea, was behaving very cautiously, and at the Parliamentary Party meeting of 28 June 1950 it was agreed to postpone debate until negotiations were further advanced. [15] At the Parliamentary Party meeting on 11 July it was unanimously agreed that the SPD representatives should participate in the committee concerned with negotiating the Schuman Plan. The action followed an interview between Adenauer and Schumacher earlier that day. The six members nominated were Drs Koch, Luetkens and Veit, Professor Nölting from the Bundestag, and Herr Odenthal and Dr Georg August Zinn of the Bundesrat. [16] These six representatives participated from 17 July. On 14 July the Parliamentary Party agreed to a Parliamentary Party Commission being set up on the Schuman Plan – membership included Imig, Freitag, Schöne and Bärsch. [17] Despite objections to some elements of the plan, the SPD attitude towards the question of European integration was fairly positive at this time, and on 26 July 1950 the SPD supported an all-party motion for a Federal European Pact (the Communists voted against). This pact was to provide for the establishment of a directly elected supranational federal union with legislative, executive and judicial functions, directed at bringing about European economic unity, a common European foreign policy, equal rights for all European peoples and basic freedoms for European citizens. [18]

At the seventh sitting of the Council of Europe on 14 August 1950, Professor Nölting spoke for the SPD on the Schuman Plan. [19] In general, he welcomed the idea of the plan, but indicated that the SPD was unable to take up any position, since negotiations were still only at a preliminary stage. There were, however, in the view of the SPD, three preconditions for their approval.

The first was that production must not be restricted.

The second was that arrangements must be made to ensure that all the participating national economies started off at the same level and with equal chances of development. This implied the abolition of the IAR and the lifting of production ceilings.

The third precondition was the representation of trade unionists both in the negotiations and in the final institutions.

On the institutional question, Nölting rather surprisingly came out against the interposition of a Council of Ministers desired by the Benelux countries, and in favour of a supranational High Authority albeit with a strong parliament. The SPD abstained in the final vote.

Developing hostility towards the plan

In two interviews, one on 5 September 1950 and one on 24 October, Schumacher had become much cooler towards the idea of the Schuman Plan, though he still maintained that his final attitude was dependent on the shape of the treaty. This was due not so much to the way the Schuman Plan negotiations were progressing, as to the French plans on West German rearmament. These greatly increased SPD hostility to both the French government, which initiated the suggestions, and the Adenauer government, which was prepared to accept them. [20] In a speech to the Parliamentary Party on 1 November 1950, Schumacher's attitude had further hardened. In this speech he expressed deep suspicion of the National Assembly's demand that acceptance of the Schuman Plan be a precondition for a West German military contribution and at the lack of details provided by the respective governments. 'One can say that the prospects for the Schuman Plan have never been as poor as at present.'[21]

The SPD voted unanimously against a motion in the Bundestag which urged conclusion of the Schuman Plan negotiations according to the Council of Europe recommendations.[22] Professor Nölting reflected this hostile attitude in a second speech to the Council of Europe on the Schuman Plan on 21 November 1950.[23]

Intransigent opposition

As negotiations drew to a close and the exact details became known, Schumacher grew ever more intransigently opposed. In a speech in Hanover on 24 February 1951, Schumacher criticised the plan in resounding terms. Although he repeated the by now familiar arguments on the necessity for West German equality in the new institution, and the preservation of the nationalisation option, the depth of his suspicion of France was new and contrasted sharply with his attitude at the time of the plan's announcement. This change can be traced to the new suspicions aroused by the highly emotionally charged issue of West German rearmament. There was also a new emphasis on technical details now that the details of the plan had become known. Ironically, in view of his stigmatising the Schuman Plan as cartellistic, Schumacher was concerned to defend the coal sales cartel of the Ruhr. In doing this, Schumacher was uneasily aware that he was defending the interests of the Ruhr Magnates as well as preserving the economic interests of the German worker.

In the following weeks Schumacher made a series of impassioned speeches against the Schuman Plan and called for new elections.[24] Adenauer's position was, however, strengthened by a decision of the French government, made public in a letter from Robert Schuman to Adenauer on 18 April 1951, that the Ruhr Authority would cease to exist on the ratification of the Schuman Plan.[25]

In reply, the SPD Executive published a seven-point memorandum on 20 April 1951.

1   There must be complete legal and political equality in the institutions and workings of the Schuman Plan.
2   It must include all democratic Europe, including Britain and Scandinavia.
3   There must be planning at both a European and a national level.
4   Representation in all international institutions must be on the basis of importance and volume of production.

5 There must be a democratic parliament to control the Executive.

6 National economies must be allowed to develop without interference from power politics.

7 Workers must be accorded parity of representation. [26]

At the local level some SPD members were, however, in favour of the plan, and the Party Executive felt obliged, at its meeting on 1 April, to pass a resolution criticising a statement by Wilhelm Kaisen in favour of the plan. [27] It took no action against Otto Bach, the Berlin Senator, who was making similar speeches. [28] In the Berlin section of the party, support for West German entry was not restricted to Reuter and Bach, but encompassed a substantial minority of the party, and Ollenhauer met a great deal of opposition to the standpoint of the Party Executive on the Schuman Plan when he spoke to the conference of the Berlin section in mid-May.

The biggest obstacle to Schumacher's policy of opposition was not internal party opponents, but the attitude of the trade union leaders. The DGB published a communiqué on 7 May, expressing its approval of the Coal and Steel Community with certain provisos. The main provisos were that trade union interests should be safeguarded at all levels and full employment and a high standard of living protected. Furthermore, the relics of the occupation status must be swept away and Law no. 27 must be interpreted in a way which gave Germany full equality. The communiqué concluded with a demand for a commission, with 50 per cent German membership, to be set up to make new arrangements after the break up of the coal sales agency. [29] The attitude of the DGB Central Committee did not go entirely unopposed. Viktor Agartz, Director of the DGB's Economic Institute and a representative of the extreme Left of the trade union movement came out strongly against the plan in a pamphlet 'Dass steht im Schumanplan'. [30] He demonstrated that German steel sales would suffer through decartellisation and (surprisingly for a trade unionist) through the burden of equalising wages and fringe benefits. There was also some opposition from the Metal Workers Union and its President, and SPD Deputy, Walter Freitag claimed, in a radio talk on 11 May, that apprehension over the division of coal supplies in the Community and the Saar issue prevented the union from approving the plan. [31]

Schumacher considered the attitude of those trade union leaders who supported the treaty as disloyal. In his view, the SPD was to supply the political leadership. He therefore made his most comprehensive attack on the Coal and Steel Community to a trade union audience in Gelsenkirchen on 25 May. This speech represented a last great attempt to win over trade union opinion. Reprinted by the Party Executive as 'Fifty years with

57

bound hands' it is still one of the most damaging attacks by any politician on an institution of the European Community.[32] Its economic content owes a lot to Professor Fritz Baade (see contribution by Baade in *Probleme des Schuman Plans*)[33] and Agartz, but the combination of economics, politics and biting rhetoric is quintessential Schumacher.

As the title suggests, Schumacher's main attack was concentrated on the fifty year duration of the Treaty, and he suggested, as an alternative, a provisional plan for five years. Schumacher failed to convince the DGB except for the intellectuals like Agartz. Co-determination, promised to them by Adenauer in return for their support, was what attracted them. The Consultative Committee of the ECSC, in which employers and trade unions were to be granted equal representation, seemed to them like co-determination altered to fit the international scene.[34]

The debates

The first debate on the Schuman Plan actually took place in the Bundesrat on 27 June 1951. Professor Karl Schiller spoke in a dual capacity as rapporteur of the Economics Committee of the Bundesrat and as mover of the Hamburg Resolution.[35]

The Hamburg Resolution, while superficially similar to the famous seven points, did not contain a request for planning at an international level or for equal representation of trade unionists. It did, however, lie fairly close to the official policy of the party. Schiller concluded by requesting the Bundesrat to accord neither an 'unbedingtes Ja' or an 'unbedingtes Nein' (unqualified Yes or No) to the treaty.

Wilhelm Kaisen, a supporter of the Hamburg Resolution, was however more positive about the Schuman Plan.[36] He referred specifically to the hopes aroused in Germany with the announcement of the plan linked German development since 1945 with the progress of the European idea. While Kaisen had some reservations, his approach was quite different: 'we must help the Federal government. That is the point of the whole thing.'[37] All three sections of the Hamburg Resolution were defeated. Bremen, Lower Saxony, Hamburg and Hesse voted for the resolution, with Berlin abstaining.[38]

If the SPD leadership had been fairly successful in getting the Länder leaders behind it, it had much more difficulty in convincing foreign socialist parties. A revealing insight into these difficulties is furnished by the minutes of a conference on the Schuman Plan, held under the auspices of the Founding Conference of the Socialist International at Frankfurt on Main on 27–28 June 1951. While the SPD was strongly represented by

Wehner, Luetkens and Nölting, very few people turned up from other parties at this meeting. Salamon Grumbach, who in many ways had attempted to act as a bridge between the SPD and SFIO, referred to a discussion between himself, Mollet and Gazier of the SFIO, and Schumacher, Ollenhauer and Heine. At this discussion the SFIO representatives had asked which articles of the Schuman Plan specifically prevented socialisation and workers' participation, and which articles had led to the fear of unemployment. The SPD representatives had been unable to specify the articles. [39]

The final resolutions of the Conference did, however, mirror some of the SPD objections. It stated:

1 That the treaty should give no power to any of its bodies to interfere with or make impossible the nationalisation or socialisation of the coal and steel industries.

2 That the treaty should not permit the planning measures of the Schuman Plan to be frustrated by free enterprise or liberal economies in individual countries. The participating governments must be in a position to exercise an effective control of productive forces in their own countries.

3 That an addition should be made to the treaty in order to provide for safeguards and measures in conformity with Article 20 of the Schuman Plan for an effective policy of full employment.

4 That an effective democratic control of the High Authority be established and that further adequate participation of the trade unions be established going beyond the arrangements for representation on the consultative committee.

5 That no discrimination be allowed in relation to any one of the participating countries which implied in relation to the Federal Republic, the dissolution of the Ruhr Authority before the entry into force of the Schuman Plan, the repeal of production ceilings and further the repeal of the one-sided decartellisation regulations. In its investment policy the High Authority must give due regard to Germany's special circumstances.

6 That with regard to coal and steel production and distribution, the closest co-operation should be established with the United Kingdom and the Scandinavian countries for the benefit of Europe as a whole. [40]

The resolution on Europe passed by the whole conference of the Socialist International was so general and anodyne as to be almost meaningless. Nevertheless, the SPD alone abstained on the defence section. [41]

The first reading

The first reading of the treaty setting up the European Coal and Steel Community took place on 12 July 1951. The government case was presented, as in the previous Bundesrat debate, by Chancellor Adenauer personally. Adenauer was at pains to stress the reciprocal concessions made by all the governments of the six countries. This long process of inter-governmental compromise rendered futile the introduction of amendments designed to alter sections of articles. The treaty was in his view essentially dynamic: the integration of coal and steel would lead to further integration. While Adenauer regretted the UK decision not to take part in the ECSC, he felt that the UK would wish to be associated with it. He pointed out, to the obvious discomfiture of the SPD that large sections of French heavy industry had opposed the plan. The surrender of sovereignty involved in the Schuman Plan would, Adenauer concluded, strike a heavy blow at nationalism. [42]

The SPD had introduced a resolution (Drucksache 2484) requesting that the second reading be postponed until five sets of preconditions had been met: [43]

1   Binding declarations from all the relevant foreign powers that the Ruhr Authority, the Allied Coal and Steel Groups, the restriction of coal and steel production would be abolished by the entry into force of the ECSC.

2   An additional protocol, added to the transitional agreement, making arrangements for more investment in Germany.

3   The restoration of the 'Verbundwirtschaft' and the organisation of a new coal sales organisation.

4   Sufficient German control over the export of coal and steel to ensure the necessary imports of food and raw materials.

5   Clarification of the position of the Saar. This clarification would imply a binding declaration by the French government that German acceptance of the Saar status quo was not a precondition of French participation in the plan.

Carlo Schmid, who made the main SPD speech, rejected the charge that SPD policy was negative by drawing a parallel with the refusal of the SPD to accept the Allied constitutional design for West Germany in its entirety – a refusal which had been the precondition of the establishment of a viable West Germany. [44] Schmid's speech was concerned with the political aspects of the Schuman Plan; the economic aspects were presented by Henssler.

The main thrust of Schmid's argument was directed against the logic of sectoral integration. Any action by the High Authority in the coal and steel fields was bound to have repercussions in other sectors which would have to be dealt with by national governments — a process which could only lead to confusion. It would also be impossible for any government to have an economic policy which was not ultimately dependent on the prior decisions of the High Authority. The parliaments of the various countries would have no way of checking the High Authority, yet its actions would affect areas for which they were constitutionally responsible.

The High Authority as constituted represented a coalition of five countries without large supplies of coal with one that did, Germany. The difficulties this caused would be difficult to remove, since there was no revision clause in the treaty — the Versailles Treaty, after all, had had a revision clause. What the SPD wanted was 'not a supranational organ with independent powers of its own but rather an international co-operative and co-ordinating organisation responsible to parliamentary control'. [45]

Schmid assigned little importance to the Council of Ministers as a defender of German interests. There was also little comfort to be drawn from an Assembly which was restricted to dismissing the High Authority *en bloc* and that by a two-thirds majority. Schmid claimed sensibly enough that it was impossible to imagine the assembly doing this on German initiative.

Schmid closed his speech on an authentic Schumacher note, by rejecting a policy of preconditions, and he referred again to Versailles, pointing out that the German rewards for fulfilling the preconditions had never materialised. West Germany was not in a position to enter an undertaking like the ECSC since it would tend to freeze the status quo — a status quo which had as one of its main features a divided Germany.

> For the inequality of the founding relationships affects, whether one likes it or not, the rules established by the treaties. For this reason, in the present situation Germany ought not to conclude such treaties, treaties which do more than regulate the *modus vivendi* and create *faits accomplis*. Otherwise, when eventually formal equality is reached, it will be meaningless. [46]

Fritz Henssler, a close confidant of Schumacher's, concentrated on the economic aspects of the treaty. [47] While his speech was generally defensive, since it was in the economic field that the Federal government could point to concrete benefits, he presented the SPD case against signing treaties when one is weak with great clarity:

it seems better at the present time to shoulder one-sided burdens than to accept less onerous burdens imposed on a treaty basis, since we can defend ourselves against a policy directed against us, and our opponent must have the strength to see it through. He will not always possess the necessary means or strength of will to do this and, precisely because they realised that it will be impossible to force us to continue to accept the occupation regime, they want us to take over a half or a quarter of the burden voluntarily for fifty years. [48]

The SPD motions were heavily defeated.

In the months that followed the first reading, most attention was focussed on the rearmament debate, and the Schuman Plan was next discussed at a meeting of the Parliamentary Party on the eve of the second reading. This meeting of the Parliamentary Party on 8 January, held under the Chairmanship of Ollenhauer, due to the onset of Schumacher's fatal illness, proved to be an inauspicious one for the party leadership. [49] Ollenhauer opened the meeting by saying that he supported and would advance the views of the Party Executive in the second reading, which would take place the following day. [50] Hermann Brill then demanded that Ollenhauer specify the main points that he would make in order to let him, Brill, make up his mind. [51] Ollenhauer indicated seven main areas that he would dwell on: 'no junktim', the applicability of the Schuman Plan to the whole of Germany, 'Gleichberechtigung', the participation of all European states, real possibilities of revision, democratic control and workers' participation.

At this point, Heiland referred to a declaration by Brill, announced by d.p.a., (German Press Agency), and demanded an explanation. Brill denied that he had made a declaration — in fact he made it later that day and claimed that the leadership had not sufficiently consulted the whole Party on the issue. Furthermore, the position of the Party Executive had not always been clear and free from ambivalence. He then spoke darkly about bolshevist methods in the party and demanded a return to the democratic socialist tradition of Kautsky. [52] In his view, the Schuman Plan ought to be accepted to preserve peace and avoid economic misery. For internal political resons, however, he would have to oppose the treaty. He would therefore vote for Article I but reject the treaty as a whole.

Ollenhauer, visibly annoyed, rejected the charges of bolshevist methods. He pointed out that the question had been discussed in Berlin, Bremen and Hamburg and that party members in all three areas had voted overwhelmingly for rejection of the treaty. [53] When Brill was called once again to state his position he said that he would vote against the treaty but would abstain with regard to the SPD resolution.

Brill made a public declaration to the press later in the day. It was a bitter and pointed attack on the policy of the party leadership. Opposition to the Schuman Plan was limited, he claimed, to a tiny proportion of the party functionaries. The broad masses were instinctively for it. He pointed out that the Berlin Senate had voted unanimously for participation in the ECSC. Hamburg had only rejected the economic aspects of the plan. The Bremen Assembly had equally been enthusiastic about many parts of it. This did not, of course, meet Ollenhauer's point that the party, as distinct from the governmental organisations in these areas, had rejected the plan. Furthermore, all the other socialist parties of the Six were for it.

More damagingly, he pointed out that prominent SPD members nominated by the Parliamentary Party had taken part in the negotiations. Luetkens and Zinn had participated in the legal committee; Nölting on that relating to production; Koch on investment and credit; Nölting on coal and Schöne on iron and steel. The line taken by the Executive had been inconsistent and continually changing – no attempt had been made to present alternatives. The argument that the ECSC was a cartel was ridiculous, since it was not an agreement between private interests. Due to his internationalism fostered in the concentration camp he approved of the general idea of the Schuman Plan. He would, however, reject the treaty because of the way it had been negotiated by the government. There had been no participation by the Bundestag and insufficient information had been disseminated by the negotiating committees. The Saar issue had been badly handled by Adenauer and not enough had been done to bring Britain in.

> Thus the internal policy of the Federal government in respect to the Schuman Plan is a chain of neglect, failure and mistakes, the silencing of facts and burdens. The government's policy is characterised by lack of judgment and imagination enough to justify rejecting it on internal political grounds alone. [54]

Despite the attack on the government, the declaration as a whole represented a clear attack on the party leadership on the eve of an important debate. Luckily for the leadership, Brill was very much an outsider and had no consistent body of support in the Parliamentary Party.

The ratification debates

The SPD prepared four resolutions for the second reading of the ratifica-

tion of the Schuman Plan. The first resolution asked for the postpone-
ment of the third reading until the discrimination engendered by Law
no. 27 had disappeared. The second resolution asked for assurances regarding unemployed miners and steel workers. The third resolution demanded an agreement with the other five countries extending the ECSC to
Berlin, a report on the ministerial discussions of the Council of Europe on
the undesirable effects of the ECSC on the Saar issue, the final plans for
the coal sales agency, and the publication of the treaties designed to sweep
away the last vestiges of the occupation. The fourth resolution incorporated a series of points aimed at securing 'Gleichberechtigung' in the economic field for Germany. The Communist Party (KPD), much to the
SPD's embarrassment, also produced a resolution deploring the Schuman
Plan as a danger to peace. Few new arguments were produced in support
of these resolutions in the second and third readings and they were badly
defeated, being supported only by the KPD and some members of the
extreme right like von Thadden. The Refugees Party (BHE) abstained. [55]
   In these two crucial debates, the weakness of the SPD without Schumacher, namely its lack of a figure comparable to Adenauer, was glaringly
obvious. This defeat was reflected in the unanimous Bundesrat ratification
of the ECSC almost without debate on 1 February 1952. [56]
   The opposition of the party leadership to the Schuman Plan continued
unabated (see Ollenhauer's address to the Parliamentary Party meeting on
5 February, after the Bundesrat vote and the Dortmund Aktionsprogramm). [57] The longest attack on the Schuman Plan was published by
the Party Executive in 1953. Entitled *Götterdammerung beim Schuman
plan*, the cover depicts a starving man crawling over a devastated Germany. [58] The text is a compendium of all the SPD's complaints against the
ECSC and is designed to demonstrate how the worst fears of the party
have been realised. The most piquant section is the attempt to explain
why SPD members taught from the cradle to distrust the Ruhr Magnates
should in fact support their policy on the ECSC. The answer given is
ingenious: cartels are needed for modernisation of technology and security of employment and, in any case, there would be no problem if the SPD
policy of nationalisation were adopted. [59] After 1953, the SPD attitude
gradually changed from hostility to wholehearted espousal.

Conclusion

The SPD position, then, had changed from benevolent neutrality to intransigent opposition in the course of the realisation of the Schuman

64

initiative. There were, I think, four main reasons for this. The first was the non-participation of Britain: Schumacher never wavered in his view that a rump Germany tied to the Six and cut off from the progressive north, particularly Britain, would be inimical to the development of a socialist Germany. Secondly, he was intensely suspicious of France, a prejudice shared by practically the whole party. Thirdly, there was the great influence exercised by Henssler, Baade, Nölting and Agartz. Under the influence of these 'experts' Schumacher really believed that the Schuman Plan denied German economic equality. This would lead to an economic and therefore, with his view of Germany, a political 'Götterdammerung'. The influence of Henssler, the party's most powerful figure in North Rhine—Westphalia, explains his otherwise surprising defence of the coal sales cartel. Lastly, there was the connection established between Adenauer, French agreement to the Schuman Plan, and the European Defence Community (EDC).

The non-participation of Britain was important, indeed fundamental, since it was the non-participation of Britain that cooled Schumacher's initial enthusiasm and turned it into an attitude of watchful hostility. The intransigent nature of his opposition derived, however, from the remaining three grounds, his suspicion of the French, his economic fears and the connection with rearmament. These fears interacted with Schumacher's realisation that the negotiations were very probably going to succeed. By this time he was obsessed with the knowledge that he only had a short time to live. It was to him, therefore, absolutely essential that West Germany should not become a member of an organisation which placed decisions affecting the direction to be taken by West Germany in the future not only in conservative hands, but French conservative hands at that. The question as to whether or not the Schuman Plan rendered nationalisation impossible is a particularly clear illustration of this point.

While still important the reunification issue, the Saar, and the vestiges of the occupation regime were only secondary themes. In my view, they would have been ignored if Britain had been behind the plan, and if Germany's economic interests, including the freedom to nationalise, had been more obviously defended. The attack on the supranational form of the ECSC and the preference expressed for looser co-operative forms sprang more from suspicion of the motives of Germany's partners than deep-rooted objections to supranational forms, since the SPD complaint against the Council of Europe had been that it was not 'European' – that is, not supranational – enough. The criticism of the lack of powers of the parliament reflected the SPD's deep and abiding commitment to democracy, but Schumacher was always enough of a realist not to make the question of democracy the sticking point. The underlying strategy of an opposition based on nationalism, or, more accurately, opposition with a nationalist tone, remained unchanged. While Adenauer's comparison of the SPD with Hugenberg was overdone, the SPD had laid itself open to this charge by its talk of a second Versailles and characterisation of Adenauer as a tool of the Allies. Its general strategy of opposition on foreign policy issues was now proving a bit of a bent reed.

As we saw in the last chapter, once the treaty had been ratified the SPD had little choice other than to accept the consequences, committed as it was to parliamentary procedures. It is noticeable that there was no controversy over the sending of representatives to the Common Assembly of the Coal and Steel Community as there had been over the question of sending representatives to the Consultative Assembly of the Council of Europe. Democratically impeccable as this attitude was, it was hardly a tactic that would be expected to attract mass support to the party. The chances of attracting such support had in any case been weakened by the aggressive way in which Schumacher treated those, like Kaisen, who disagreed with him within the party, and important allies like the leadership of the DGB. Similarly. damaging was the failure to win any significant external support for SPD's European policies, even from fellow socialists. Not only was this a blow to the socialist self-esteem of the party leadership, but it was a major electoral handicap in a situation where Adenauer was able to attract so much visible foreign support.

Secure in the support of the Allies and the trade unions, and aided by the industrial boom occasioned by the outbreak of the Korean War, Adenauer looked impregnable. The SPD had, in any case, already transferred most of its hopes of success to the defence field. This was an area where antipathy to the government's policy was not confined to a few theoreticians and functionaries, but seemed to be shared by the mass of the population.

Notes

[1] *The Times*, 10 May 1950.
[2] Ibid. See L'Année Politique, 1950, pp. 306—7, for full text.
[3] William Diebold, *The Schuman Plan — a Study in Economic Co-operation, 1950—59*, New York 1959, p. 11. My account of the origins of the ECSC relies very heavily on Diebold, who in turn relies on Pierre Gerbet 'La Genèse du Plan Schuman', *Revue Française de Science Politique*, September 1956, pp. 525—53.

4 W. Diebold, op. cit., pp. 16–19.

5 P. Gerbet, op. cit., p. 553.

6 K. Adenauer, op. cit., vol. 1, p. 257.

7 K. Adenauer, op. cit., vol. 1, pp. 258–60. Contrast with his earlier offer, which made Fanco–German union conditional on the return of the Saar to Germany (Chapter 11, p. 53).

8 *Die Neue Zeitung*, 12 May 1950.

9 *Frankische Tagespost*, 15 May 1950.

10 *Volkszeitung am Wochenende*, Schleswig–Holstein, 20 May 1950.

11 *Protokoll des Hamburger Parteitages*, pp. 72–6.

12 Ibid., p. 76.

13 Ibid., p. 274.

14 *Sopade* no. 899, July 1950, pp. 84–5.

15 *Protokoll der Fraktionssitzung*, 28 June 1950.

16 *Protokoll der Fraktionssitzung*, 11 July 1950.

17 *Protokoll der Fraktionssitzung*, 14 July 1950.

18 G. Siegler, *Europäische politische Eingung*, Bonn 1968, p. 1.

19 Council of Europe, *Consultative Assembly, 14 August 1950*, pp. 400–4 (E. Nölting).

20 Interview with Fritz Sternberg, 5 September 1950 (filed under Q7); interview, 24 October, *Neuer Vorwärts*, 27 October 1950.

21 Speech reprinted by the Party Executive as 'Das Volk soll entscheiden', Bonn, November 1950. See also *Sopade* no. 903, pp. 4–9.

22 Deutscher Bundestag, *Verhandlungen*, 1 November 1950, p. 3754.

23 Council of Europe, *Consultative Assembly, 21 November 1950*, pp. 1368–9 (E. Nölting).

24 For Hanover speech see *Sopade* 907, pp. 8–10. For succeeding speakers see *Neuer Vorwärts*, 2 March 1951, 16 March 1951; *FAZ*, 2 April 1951; *NV*, 25 March 1951, 4 May 1951. See especially speech to Small Party Conference on 31 March 1951, reprinted by the Party Executive as 'Macht Europa Stark' Bonn 1951. This contains a strong plea for new elections.

25 K. Adenauer, op. cit., vol. 1, pp. 358–9.

26 Q17, Schuman Plan.

27 *Die Welt*, 4 April 1951. Although Kaisen received a personal vote of confidence from the local SPD at its annual conference, the majority of the local party supported the policy of the Party Executive on the ECSC. *NV* no. 25, 1951.

28 See letter from Sascha Merz to Schumacher, 1 April 1951, complaining about Otto Bach's pro ECSC speeches in Berlin. Filed under N2 (Correspondence of the Party Executive with the Berlin section of the party).

Attached to this letter is a letter demanding explanation from Heine-Bach but there is no reply.

[29] *Die Neue Zeitung*, 8 May 1951; *Hannoversche Presse*, 11 May 1951.

[30] V. Agartz, *Dass steht im Schuman plan*, Cologne 1951; DGB *Vorstand Industriekurier*, 19 June 1951.

[31] *Die Neue Zeitung*, 12 May 1951.

[32] '50 Jahre mit gebundenen Händen', Bonn 1951, pp. 1–19. See also *Die Neue Zeitung*, 25 May 1951.

[33] F. Baade in 'Probleme des Schuman Plans' *Kieler Vorträge*, Neue Folge 2, Kiel 1951, pp. 21–35.

[34] Interview (Summer 1967) with Hans vom Hoff, in charge of DGB negotiations with the ECSC and later member of the High Authority.

[35] Deutscher Bundesrat, *Verhandlungen* 27 June 1951, pp. 448–50 (K. Schiller, Hamburg Antrag Br. Drucksache N. 470/2/51). This in turn is based on 'Hamburger Denkschrift zum Schuman Plan' by Professor Ritschel, issued by the SPD Party Executive as '13 Punkte zum Schuman Plan' 1951.

[36] Deutscher Bundesrat, *Verhandlungen*, 27 June 1951, pp. 451–3 (W. Kaisen).

[37] Ibid., p. 452 (W. Kaisen).

[38] Ibid., pp. 455–7.

[39] *Protokoll* of this meeting, filed under J42 (the Schuman Plan).

[40] Ibid.

[41] *Sopade* no. 911, July 1951, p. 29.

[42] Deutscher Bundestag, *Verhandlungen*, 12 July 1951, pp. 6499–502 (K. Adenauer).

[43] Deutscher Bundestag *Verhandlungen* – Anlagen (Supplements) Vol. 2 Drs. Nos. 2301, 2500, 1951.

[44] Deutscher Bundestag Verhandlungen, 12 July 1951, pp. 6510–11.

[45] Ibid, p. 6514.

[46] Ibid, p. 6520 (C. Schumid).

[47] Ibid, pp. 6535–9 (F. Henssler).

[48] Ibid, p. 6539.

[49] See *Protokoll der Fraktionssitzung*, 8 January 1952.

[50] Ibid, p. 1.

[51] Ibid, p. 1.

[52] Brill's experiences in Buchenwald and, after the war, in Thuringia had made him almost paranoic about communism.

[53] This was the factor that circumscribed the power of the Bürgermeisterflügel.

[54] *Die Welt*, 9 January 1952.

[55] For an analysis of this debate see my London Ph.D. thesis 'The SPD and European Integration 1949–57 – A Study of Opposition in Foreign Affairs', pp. 101–4.

[56] See Deutscher Bundesrat, *Verhandlungen*, 1 February 1952, p. 134. However, Haas (op. cit., p. 132) is totally wrong to conclude that this proves the SPD was not opposed to the ECSC, and his claim that the opposition of the party leadership was only 'Scheinopposition' (opposition of appearances) is false.

[57] See Chapter 4, note 102.

[58] *Götterdämmerung beim Schumanplan*, SPD Party Executive (PV), Bonn 1953.

[59] Ibid, p. 14.

4 The SPD, the European Defence Community and Western European Union

The question of West German participation in the Western defence effort was one of enormous political and strategic complexity, and it dominated inter-Allied diplomacy from 1950 to 1955.[1] It was first raised officially by Allied military planners shortly after the signing of the NATO treaty on 4 April 1949. A long term plan was drawn up to indicate the level of forces that would be needed to defend Europe against an all-out conventional attack. It was very clear from this plan that forces of the required magnitude could not be supplied by Britain, France and the smaller allies, and that the forces could only be provided by the arming of West Germany. Following this report, the United States Army General Staff drafted an outline plan for the creation of a German force in autum1949.[2]

The first official West German comment was made by Adenauer on 11 November 1949 in an interview with the French newspaper *L'Est Republicain*, in which he indicated his willingness to accede to German rearmament provided it was as part of a European army.

> If a common Supreme Command could be created, the Federal Republic would be willing at an appropriate time to integrate itself in to a European defence system.[3]

This interview attracted surprisingly little attention, but one given on 3 December 1949 to the European correspondent of the *Cleveland Plain Dealer*, in which he advanced very much the same argument, attracted world wide attention.[4] Adenauer chose the correspondent of the *Cleveland Plain Dealer* for two main reasons, both of which indicate how subtle a path he was treading. Firstly, it was one of the few newspapers regularly read by President Truman, whose support was essential to Adenauer. Secondly, its European reporter spoke no German, a circumstance which made it possible for Adenauer later to deny that he had said what was attributed to him, when world reaction proved less positive than he had hoped. Adenauer then modified his position, stressing that he did not personally desire German rearmament, but if it were forced on Germany

71

then it ought to be in the framework of a European army. He was opposed, however, to the idea of Germans being recruited into non-German
contingents or to their serving as mercenaries.[5]

The initial position

The SPD response is best conveyed in Schumacher's comment: 'At the
present moment we have enough worries, people should not bother us
with this sort of thing.'[6]

Adenauer maintained his reserved support for West German rearmament in the Bundestag debate of 16 December 1949. While he held that
West German rearmament was unthinkable, he added that if European
security ultimately required a West German contribution, then the formation of a German army within a European one might be considered. Erich
Ollenhauer, speaking in Schumacher's absence, regretted both that the
rearmament issue had been raised at all and that Adenauer had chosen to
make his first declaration outside the Bundestag. The SPD were, he said,
not even prepared to consider West German rearmament, since German
security was the responsibility of the Western powers and West Germany
was in any case prevented from taking measures in defence of its own
security under the terms of the Occupation Statute. In his view, the
setting up of armed police units in East Germany hardly constituted a
sufficient reason for abrogating the exclusive responsibility of the Western
powers for the defence of West Germany. Instead of encouraging nationalist and military circles at home and raising doubts about Germany's
intentions abroad, the West German government should consolidate West
Germany's freedom and social strength. Such a policy would be more
likely to contribute to a peaceful settlement of the Cold War than increasing the tensions between the occupying powers; tensions which had led to
Germany's division and now impeded its reunification.[7]

However, it was not until 25 June 1950, the date of the invasion of
South Korea by forces from the communist North that the question of a
West German defence force became a live issue. In an important speech on
25 July, the United States High Commissioner, John McCloy, stated publicly what he had asserted privately, that it would be necessary to give the
West Germans the means of defending themselves against aggression because of the changed situation after the outbreak of the Korean war.[8]

Schumacher's first important pronouncement, which foreshadowed in
its main outlines later, more comprehensive attacks, was made in Hanover
on 31 July. In this speech Schumacher rejected the parallel between the

German and Korean situations. The Western Allies had a secure presence in West Germany and it was this presence that deterred the Russians rather than any contribution West Germany could make. Rearmament was in any case unthinkable while West Germany lacked sovereignty. It was much more important that the Western Allies develop a strategy which did not condemn West Germany to becoming merely a battleground. The real danger, in any case, was not military but social. It was poor social conditions that offered the best opportunity for communist expansion.[9]

The first real public debate took place at the August session of the Council of Europe. André Philip, the most European member of the SFIO, demanded the creation of a European army, financed by a European fund, created out of European taxes, which would include a West German contingent.[10] Paul Reynaud then called on the West German delegation (this was its first appearance in Strasbourg) to support West German rearmament.

Carlo Schmid, who spoke for the SPD, replied in the negative. The SPD would refuse to agree to West German rearmament so long as 'Europe' — that is, a European supranational political authority — had not come into being. It would in any case be impossible to demand a contribution from a West German goverment which was not free to undertake its own engagements on the international level. There were in his view four main objections to West German rearmament.

1 If the Allies were as short of modern arms as they proclaimed, how would the West German troops be equipped?
2 It would provide an excellent pretext for a Russian invasion.
3 It would be regarded as intolerable by the mass of the population of Germany's neighbouring states.
4 In a weak state such as the Federal Republic, a re-created army would have too much power. If a European army preceded a European government, it could only be a coalition army, an army for the achievement in common of the disparate national interests of members who would feel the effects of any reversal of alliances.[11]

Attention ought, in Schmid's view, to have been concentrated on raising living standards and creating a European political authority.

Winston Churchill's motion on 11 August, that the Council demand the formation of a European army under a European Minister of Defence, was adopted by 89 votes to 5 with 27 abstentions. The SPD voted against and the Labour Party abstained.[12]

Schumacher made a major policy statement at a press conference on 23 August 1950.[13] This statement had been unanimously approved by the Party Executive at its July meeting. Schumacher's first concern was to demonstrate that remilitarisation must not be viewed in purely military terms. Its political consequences must also be considered. Schumacher completely rejected any parallel with the Korean situation. The East German People's Police would only attack if the Russians had decided on World War III, since the People's Police alone would make no impression on the Western occupation forces. By offering to rearm, Adenauer had sacrificed his strongest bargaining counter without achieving any concessions from the Western Allies. In any case, as Schumacher pointed out, the West Germans alone could make no significant defence contribution, and even integrated European forces would not suffice. What was needed was the power of world democracy, especially that of the United States, or else Germany would merely become the initial battleground.

> The German military effort only makes sense if world democracy protects Germany offensively against the East, that is, protects Germany from the worst of the destruction and intends seeking, in reply to a Russian attack, the decisive military course of action east of Germany. That is the first and intrinsically the only condition, for the Yes and No to German rearmament. The great ability and will of the USA and the other democracies must become more visible here in Germany, that is, it is not necessarily a question of an increase in the number of occupation troops by one or two tank divisions, but the massive centralisation of forces. It is necessary to rebuild confidence in Europe and Germany by the concentration of decisive military forces on the Eastern borders of the Federal Republic ... the decisive tactical mistake is an inadequate German rearmament which releases the American and the Great Powers as a whole from their obligation to concentrate massive military forces in West Germany. [14]

Schumacher also stressed the necessity for raising living standards in order to give the ordinary citizen the feeling of having something to defend. He concluded, however, by returning to his main point:

> ... the military counter-attack by the democracies must seek and achieve the decisive military action at the Njemen or the Vistula. [15]

At the request of the Allied High Commissioners, Adenauer submitted on 30 August 1950 a written memorandum giving his views on German security. He asked for the reinforcement of Allied troops in Germany and for the raising of a police force equivalent to the People's Police of East Germany. In return, the West German government would be prepared to sponsor the raising of German units for service in a European army, though the government remained opposed to the re-establishment of a German national army. [16] In a second memorandum to the High Commissioners, the Chancellor asked for a revision of the Occupation Statute and, in particular, a further reduction in the powers of the High Commissioners. [17]

Shortly afterwards, a meeting of the Party Executive, Control Commission, and leading Länder and parliamentary members, was held on the defence question. In the introduction to his speech Schumacher attempted to deal with the internal party criticism that he was concentrating too much on foreign policy:

> It is very clear in an occupied country that foreign policy conditions internal policy, since internal policy is an object of interest and intervention to foreign powers on our soil.

He also claimed that his policy of opposition had demonstrated to the German people the contribution a responsible opposition could make. There were three fundamental aims in the SPD's defence policy, of which only the third belonged to the classic realm of foreign policy:

1 The strengthening of the social aspects of democracy.
2 A continual struggle against authoritarianism in government policy.
3 Restoration of Germany to a full place in the international arena.

Schumacher concluded by asserting that the Allies would wish the SPD to participate in government. In a grand affirmation of his opposition strategy and his belief that rearmament was deeply unpopular, Schumacher said that any invitation to participate must be strenuously resisted. [18]

The development of plans for an EDC

As a counter to far-reaching American proposals for West German rearmament, the French Council of Ministers announced a series of proposals in the National Assembly on 24 October 1950. [19] M. Pleven proposed that there should be established a European Minister of Defence responsible to a European Assembly, which would either be the Consultative Assembly of the Council of Europe, or some body to emerge from the Assembly or some other new body to be specifically elected in accordance with an electoral law to be thereafter devised. He also proposed that there should be a European Defence Council, consisting of persons of ministerial rank and a single European defence budget; that the various participating states should contribute units from their national armies for the formation of a European army; that these units should be merged with one another at the lowest possible level, that Germany should make a contribution to this army, but that, in order to prevent the revival of mistrust, there should be no German national army and no German defence minister. The French government also wished to make agreement to the Schuman Plan a condition for the implementation of these proposals. The French National Assembly, proceeding to the vote in the early hours of 26 October, approved by 349 votes to 235 the government's declaration of policy on European defence, and by 402 to 168 the government's determination not to permit the re-creation of a German national army. Schumacher declared his opposition to these proposals in a talk on Bavarian radio on 28 October; again at a meeting in Frankfurt on 29 October; and on 1 November to the Parliamentary Party. [20]

The Parliamentary Party had had a preliminary discussion of the rearmament issue on 20 October 1950, when Schumacher reported on his talks with Adenauer and Martin Niemöller, a leading Protestant minister who had been imprisoned by the Nazis. Opposition in the Protestant church, particularly among clerics, was strong and offered the chance of a possible ally for the SPD. Schumacher stressed that Niemöller was not an unconditional pacifist. In rejecting a position of absolute pacifism for the SPD, Schumacher demonstrated clearly the limited nature of his opposition to rearmament: 'If one rejects any German contribution to security, then politics stop.' This impression is heightened by his rider: 'In this question we cannot pursue an intransigent policy.'[21]

The period in which relations between Adenauer and Schumacher could almost be described as good came to an end with the publication of the Pleven Plan on 24 October 1950. Thereafter, increasing disagreement over rearmament fed increasingly bitter arguments over the Schuman Plan. In his speech on 1 November, Schumacher rejected the coupling of the defence issue with the Schuman Plan. His distrust of the French was very apparent in his complete dismissal of the Pleven proposals and his charge that French behaviour on the Saar and over the Schuman Plan demonstrated that the French were trying to·use the European ideal for purely national ends. An absolute precondition of any German rearmament was that Germany should not be the area of initial conflict; this demanded a forward strategy on the part of the Allies. Schumacher then made one of his many demands for new elections in face of the unforeseen turn of events. [22]

In the debate following Schumacher's speech it was obvious that the Parliamentary Party was badly split. While many speakers spoke in favour of a plebiscite, others claimed that the party organisation was too confused to benefit from a plebiscite. Opinion in the Parliamentary Party also ran strongly against a too close identification with Niemöller. This opinion was, in any case, superfluous, since at their meeting in Darmstadt on 30 October Schumacher had decided that there was no basis for co-operation with Niemöller as he was too intransigently opposed to rearmament. [23] Some criticisms were also made of the party leadership. It was pointed out that the SPD's nuanced differentiation from the government's policy, of agreement in principle and opposition in practice, would be hard to put over electorally. This was likely to be even more difficult because of the divergence between north and south which was apparent at this meeting, with for instance, Birkelbach of South Hesse insisting that the question be looked at from the point of view of internal politics. This was an implicit plan for a more intransigent opposition to rearmament, since public opinion was much opposed to it. One of the most striking features of the opposition to rearmament in the churches and trade unions, as well as the SPD, was its greater strength in South Germany, particularly Hesse. At the close of the discussion, Schumacher agreed to create a committee on defence in the Party Executive. The creation of such a committee is invariably an indication that the question with which the committee is concerned is in dispute in the party. [24] However, the Parliamentary Party was able to agree unanimously to the following resolution:

> The SPD Parliamentary Party once again unanimously endorses the resolution adopted by the Party Executive and Party Committee in Stuttgart on the 17 September 1950, and declares that any German military contribution implies an alteration of the Constitution. This means that it can only be ratified by a two-thirds majority. The Parliamentary Party questions the right of the present Bundestag, elected at a time when this question had not arisen, to decide this issue. This is not a normal political question, but one that will alter the whole nature of the Federal Republic. A decision on any German military contribution is only possible on the basis of new elections. [25]

The first debate on rearmament was held in the Bundestag on 8 November 1950. Dr Adenauer welcomed the Pleven Plan, provided Britain were to play a part in it, and referred to M. Schuman's statement of 6 November which indicated that discrimination against the Germans in any European force would only be temporary. In return for their contribution, Adenauer concluded that the Germans would expect equal rights and the creation of a united front strong enough to deter Russian aggression. [26] Out-argued by Adenauer, Schumacher stressed the unacceptability of coupling defence with the Schuman Plan, Adenauer's neglect of the Saar issue, the dangers of entering into institutions which threatened German national unity, and the danger of Germany's becoming the area of initial conflict. He then made yet another plea for new elections. [27] These pleas for new elections were repeated at frequent intervals in the coming months, since the SPD was, in fact, very successful in the Land elections in Hesse and Baden-Württemberg, fought, on 19 November, on the rearmament issue, and in the Bavarian Land election on 26 November. The SPD was, not surprisingly, less successful in the Berlin elections of 3 December.

In 1951 the SPD's opposition to the government's European policy was concentrated on opposition to the ECSC. As far as the EDC was concerned, its strategy at this time was under some pressure from the left. Reimann, the KPD leader, made a request for a common front against rearmament on 27 January 1951, which was summarily rejected by Schumacher. [28] The KPD held a mammoth workers' conference against rearmament on 23-25 March 1951. Schumacher made a major speech on 8 June, rebutting the KPD charge that the SPD opposition was only 'Scheinopposition'. Aware that his position on rearmament was at best ambiguous, Schumacher concentrated on reviling the KPD as the agent of a foreign power, and devoting more attention to the Saar issue. [29] In SPD policy the Saar often tended to be a fall-back issue which was brought into prominence when things were generally quiet. Indeed, throughout 1951 there was criticism of Schumacher from both the right and left of the party. In a May interview, Kaisen condemned Schumacher's attitude as 'too extreme'. [30] Great embarrassment to Schumacher was caused by the party's foreign policy expert, Gert Luetkens, who, in a debate on 16 October 1951, declared that West Germany should not be treated as a sovereign state. [31] While such a position was implicit in some SPD statements, Luetkens' standpoint would have completely invalidated the SPD demand for 'Gleichberechtigung' and Schumacher's constant demands for the preservation of the sovereign legal rights of West Germany in any new institution. In his important speech on defence on 30 July 1950, Schumacher had indicated that West German rearmament would be acceptable if West Germany were fully sovereign. Luetkens' speech was accordingly angrily contradicted by Ollenhauer in the name of the Parliamentary Party. [32] On 15—16 December 1951, a conference of South German SPD members and trade unionists was organised by Willi Knothe Jr.

A 16-page booklet produced by the meeting, entitled 'Der Weg der Sozial-demokratie zur Völkerverständigung und zur friedlichen Vereinigung Deutschlands' called for a common front of KPD, SPD and DGB.[33] It was circulated to all party members.

On 1 January 1952, Schumacher had a stroke from which he never really recovered. Adenauer, quick to seize on an opportunity, suggested the possibility of closer co-operation between the government and opposition during the debate on the ratification of the ECSC treaty.[34] Upon the Chancellor's assurance that he intended this proposal to be taken seriously, Ollenhauer declared in the Bundestag on 16 January that any co-operation would depend on the government's willingness to provide the opposition with information throughout the course of negotiations.[35] Adenauer expressed himself ready to do this and, at meeting on 21 January, Adenauer, Ollenhauer and Schmid exchanged views on foreign policy. A communiqué stated that the talks had been informative and would be continued, but the gap was in fact too wide and progress towards co-operation was negligible.[36]

At the Parliamentary Party meeting on 15 January, Ollenhauer reported on the attitude of the Party Executive, and its decision to appeal to the Constitutional Court. This was duly approved by the Parliamentary Party. However, the depth of confusion in the party is indicated by Mertin's unanswered appeal to Ollenhauer as to whether the party was for or against rearmament. Schoettle made the most fundamental contribution when he asked what the leadership intended to do if the constitutional appeal on which it was pinning its hopes failed. It must have a clear conception of what to do then. He himself indicated that, as this was likely, it should be discussing how to shape the new army. No reply was made to this by Ollenhauer. In his summing up, Ollenhauer insisted, despite the evidence to the contrary, that the party was united. The party had to liaise more closely with the trade unions, inform itself on government plans, prepare for the Bundestag debate on defence, and press on with the constitutional objection.[37]

The constitutional battle

In order to cover the whole of the constitutional battle, some departure must be made from pure chronological order, and the next section will cover the period to 1954 dealing exclusively with the legal battle. A return to 1952 will be made in the following section to cover the parliamentary opposition to EDC.

While the SPD had occasionally resorted to the Constitutional Court while Schumacher was at the height of his powers, he saw parliament as the arena *par excellence* for the exercise of his opposition strategy. In the opposition to EDC, more attention was fixed on the Court.[38] This concentration on the legal, rather than the political, should serve to remind us of the common legal background of most prominent German politicians, including both Schumacher and Adenauer.

On 30 January 1952, when the outlines of EDC had become sufficiently clear, the members of the SPD Parliamentary Party, the constitutionally required one-third of the Bundestag, petitioned the Constitutional Court to issue a preventive injunction (Vorbeugende Normenkontrolle) decreeing that the participation of German nationals in a military establishment without an antecedent amendment to the Basic Law was *ultra vires* (Basic Law Article 24–1).[39] On 30 July 1952, the First Senate of the Constitutional Court, after oral proceedings, rejected the petition for a preventive injunction, on the grounds that judicial review applies only to statutes that have been formally enacted by parliamentary assemblies.[40]

On 19 March 1953, the EDC treaties were passed by a simple majority of the Bundestag. On 11 May 1953, 147 members of the Bundestag (that is, the SPD plus a few members of smaller parties outside the government coalition, constituting together more than the required one-third of the Bundestag), petitioned the Constitutional Court for a decision on the constitutionality of the treaties now formally ratified by the legislature. This petition in fact superseded the SPD's original complaint. Since previous decisions of the Court had held that it could not make judgements on the constitutionality of the treaties before the legislative stage had been completed it was only now possible to launch a direct attack on them.

In its petition the SPD concentrated on making clear its substantive objections to the constitutionality of the treaties under the Basic Law.[41] Its objections in this area can be considered under four main headings. The first area of objections concerned the character of the Federal Republic as a state (Staatscharakter) and its capacity under domestic law to conclude an international treaty integrating West Germany into a military alliance for a fifty year period. If West Germany possessed this capacity, would the treaty bind an all-German state if and when reunification took place? The Bonn treaty envisaged extension of the rights the Federal Republic had obtained under the EDC treaty to a unified Germany if the latter were willing to assume the treaty obligations.[42]

The second and third problem areas can be treated together. They focus on the dual question as to whether Western Germany, under International

Law, possessed military sovereignity (Wehrhoheit) and whether under national law the exercise of military powers (Wehrgewalt) belonged to the Federal State or the Länder. The Bonn Constitution failed to mention a military establishment (except by certain very oblique references) and in particular failed to include military powers in the otherwise extensive catalogue of exclusive federal powers in Article 73.

While the SPD was prepared to concede military sovereignity (Wehrhoheit) to the Federal Republic as a sovereign state, this was not to concede that the Bundestag could automatically establish armed forces without a specific designation of who is to exercise military power internally (Wehrgewalt). Nor was the SPD prepared to admit that conscription, with its attendant limitations on fundamental human rights, could be effected without specific constitutional authorisation.

It is, however, the fourth area of problems that went to the heart of the controversy. It centred on Article 24 of the Basic Law, which authorised the Federal Republic to transfer by statute sovereign rights to international organisations, and to integrate itself, for the preservation of peace, into a system of mutual collective security, thereby consenting to such limitations on its sovereign rights as would lead to and secure a peaceful and permanent order in Europe and among the nations of the world. The SPD however, questioned whether the transfer by statute covered the transfer of sovereign rights not mentioned in the Basic Law.

There was also considerable controversy as to the character of the EDC as a system of collective security under Article 24(2). The SPD contended that an EDC including a rearmed West Germany increased the danger of war, and was, therefore, not conducive to collective security. The SPD also pointed out that unarmed nations may have a vital interest in joining a system of collective security, and that the grand design of global collective security, the United Nations, does not require contributions from all its members. Lastly, the SPD held that the government had no mandate to rearm since it had not arisen in the 1949 election campaign. [43]

This plethora of legal arguments was rendered irrelevant by the result of the Federal Election of September, 1953. The coalition parties won 307 out of 497 Bundestag seats, while the SPD, with 151 seats, no longer controlled one third of the assembly. On his re-election, Dr Adenauer secured the qualified majority he needed by including the All German Party (GDP) in his coalition. However, the SPD continued to fire off briefs to the Constitutional Court, contesting the legality of this amendment, when it was obvious to all that this tactic had no hope of success. Schoettle's insistence on the necessity for the SPD to have a clear conception of what it would do when the constitutional objections failed had been ignored, and the SPD continued to send off briefs when there was no hope of success.

The pre-ratification debates

The first full-scale debate on the EDC treaty proper took place on 7–8 February 1952. In the Parliamentary Party meeting two days before the debate, the differing views of the meeting of 15 January were still apparent, though the tone of the discussion was now more intransigently against the EDC. Only relatively insignificant figures like Ritzel spoke in favour of rearmament. In his summing-up speech Ollenhauer rejected the idea of a plebiscite and also that of more extra-parliamentary agitation, which had been strongly advocated by Birkelbach in the discussion. It would also be unprofitable in his view to speculate on what should be done if the SPD position was defeated in the debate.[44] Ollenhauer was always unwilling to commit himself on future strategy as his policy was basically one of adjusting himself to the political forces dominant in the party at any one time − in this case there was the added complication of Schumacher's illness. Brandt, reflecting Reuter's fears of the declining saliency of German reunification, called for the fight against the EDC to be focussed more on German unity.[45]

On 7 February Adenauer opened the debate. He spoke of the dangers of Russian expansion, rejected any policy of neutralisation and reiterated his conviction that the only possible course for the Federal Republic, and the only hope for the reunification of Germany, lay in a close alliance with the Western Powers. This inevitably involved a contribution to the common defence. The proposed contractual agreements would give the West Germans, and the rest of Germany in the future, virtual sovereignity and democratic freedom. Turning to the Saar, he denied reports that the government would refuse to sign or initial either of the agreements until German demands about the Saar and admission to NATO had been met. He did, however, state that he was convinced (*on grounds that he was prepared to divulge only to a small committee of representatives of all parties*) that a mutually satisfactory solution for the Saar would be found. He then admitted that, temporarily at least, French actions in the Saar had shaken confidence between the two countries.[46]

The main SPD speaker, Ollenhauer, stuck pretty much to the brief he had announced at the party meeting.[47] He advanced with a fair degree of moderation the familiar arguments concerning equality, strategic security, the reunification of Germany, the impossibility of conscription without

82

an amendment to the Constitution and the need for a general election. He made very little reference to the Saar issue since, as we can see from his notes, he had anticipated that Adenauer would announce a success on this matter. [48]

Carlo Schmid had by this time, like many other South German Social Democrats, become more intransigently opposed to rearmament. In his speech he claimed that the SPD would refuse to rearm even if full equality were assured, that the contractual agreements would abolish the Occupation Statute but retain the occupation regime, and that a peace policy would only be possible between the whole of Germany and all four occupying powers. [49] Ollenhauer, in an attempt to dampen down the effect of Schmid's outburst, spoke again to explain that the party did not disagree with the principle of rearmament, only with its timing. [50]

The government resolution declaring West Germany's readiness to participate in a common defence effort was carried by 204 votes to 156. [51] Discussion at the party meeting on 12 February about the debate was very superficial: speakers were by and large preoccupied with the dangers of the Communists' drawing attention to their intransigent opposition to the treaties and the agitation in the Bavarian section of the trade unions.[52] The whole tone of the discussion was, as Schoettle pointed out, very defensive.

The same defensiveness was apparent in a radio interview on 20 February with the temporarily recovered Schumacher, who claimed that the main utility of the SPD arguments had not been in deterring or influencing the government (contrast with Schumacher's earlier declarations on opposition); rather 'they were the weapons in the dispute with the "ohne mich" sentiment, which the Communists had tried to arouse'. [53]

The episode of the Soviet notes

The voting in the debate of 7–8 February had made it clear to the Soviet Union that the EDC treaty was likely to be passed. The Soviet Union thereafter formulated a note, which was sent on 10 March 1952, proposing that Germany be united, neutralised and armed within limits to be determined by a Peace Conference. In this note the following outline for a treaty was set forth:

> *Participants:* Great Britian, the Soviet Union, the United States of America, France, Poland, Czechoslovakia, Belgium, Holland, and other governments which participated with their armed forces in the war against Germany.

83

Political Provisions:

1   Germany is re-established as a unified state, thereby an end is put to the division of Germany and a unified Germany has the possibility of development as an independent democratic peace loving State.

2   All armed forces of the occupying powers must be withdrawn from Germany not later than one year from the date of entry into force of the peace treaty. Simultaneously all foreign military bases on the territory of Germany must be liquidated.

3   Democratic rights must be guaranteed to the German people to the end that all persons under German jurisdiction without regard to race, sex, language or religion enjoy the rights of man and basic freedoms including freedom of speech, press, religious persuasion, political conviction and assembly.

4   Free activity of democratic parties and organisations must be guaranteed in Germany with the right of freedom to decide their own internal affairs, to conduct meetings and assembly, to enjoy freedom of press and of publication.

5   The existence of organisations inimical to democracy and to the maintenance of peace must not be permitted on the territory of Germany.

6   Civil and political rights equal to all other German citizens for participation in the building of peace loving democratic Germany must be made available to all former members of the German army, including officers and generals, all former Nazis, excluding those who are serving Court sentences for commission of crimes.

7   Germany obligates herself not to enter into any kind of coalition or military alliance directed against any power which took part with its armed forces in the war against Germany.

Territory; The territory of Germany is defined by the borders established by the provisions of the Potsdam Conference of the Great Powers.

Economic Provisions: No kind of limitations are imposed on Germany as to development of its peaceful economy, which must contribute to the growth of the welfare of the German people. Likewise, Germany will have no kind of limitation as regards trade with other countries, navigation and access to world markets.

Military Provisions;

1   Germany will be permitted to have its own national armed forces (land, air and sea) which are necessary for the defence of the country.

2   Germany is permitted to produce war materials and equipment, the quantity and type of which must not exceed the limitations required for the armed forces established for Germany by the peace treaty.

Germany and the United Nations Organisation: The governments concluding a peace treaty with Germany will support the application of Germany as a member of the United Nations Organisation. [54]

By this time the Western Powers were extremely reluctant to cancel their German policy and to abandon Adenauer and their own strategic plans. The High Commissioners and the Chancellor immediately let it be known that the Russian Démarche would not interrupt their discussions. [55] The identical Western replies on 25 March took exception to the imposition of neutrality on Germany and to the concession to Germany of exclusive control over German armed forces. They repeated their arguments for holding free elections as the first step in any unification and their arguments against discussing a peace treaty before such elections. They expressed the hope that a UN commission would be allowed into the Russian zone, and contested the Russian view that Germany's frontiers had been settled in Potsdam. [56]

The first SPD reaction was made public in a resolution adopted at the Parliamentary Party meeting of 11 March and published on 12 March. At this meeting the defensive tone of the last big meeting on 12 February had turned into sheer pessimism. The general conclusion was that SPD policy on the EDC lacked credibility.

Herbert Wehner reported on the Soviet note at this meeting and asked for a strictly pragmatic examination of its contents; concrete preparations for a peace treaty by Germany; the putting of concrete questions to the Western Allies; and that the Western powers identify themselves more closely with the German desire for reunification. [57]

The resolution on the Soviet note asked that the Federal government remind the Western Allies that reunification was the most urgent priority of any German government. The resolution asked secondly for a 'sachlich' (pragmatic) examination of the contents of the note by the Western Allies and that they prepare for Four Power talks on German unity, though a rider was added on the necessity of free elections. Statements made by Federal ministers rejecting the note were condemned, and a peace conference with Germany as an equal partner was demanded. The Federal government was also requested to carry out its own examination of the note. [58]

Ollenhauer criticised the Western replies on 27 March in a radio broadcast stressing the primacy of German unity. [59] Identical Soviet notes of 9 April and 25 May, were rejected by the Western Allies. [60] In the Parliamentary Party meeting of 22 April 1952, Ollenhauer reported on his unavailing protests to McCloy. A request by Stierle, an SPD backbencher, for mass action on the Soviet note and unilateral SPD negotiations with the Russians was ruled out by Wehner, who maintained that the SPD would have to content itself with pointing out the positive aspects of the note. Ollenhauer, in summing up, denied press reports that the SPD would change its position, and reported that he had refused to answer yet another letter from the KPD asking for a common front. [61]

The SPD claimed then, and indeed even into the sixties, that the Soviet note episode was one of lost opportunities for bringing about German unity. [62] The attitude of Adenauer and the Western powers at this time has been criticised by Western experts recently in much the same terms as the SPD and the Soviet offer is now generally held to have been at least partly genuine. [63] The fact remains, however, that no West German party except the KPD and certainly not the SPD, would have been prepared to proceed except on the basis of free elections. This condition remained unacceptable throughout to the USSR, though the note of 9 April, most warmly applauded by Schumacher, contained more concessions in this direction than the others. [64]

The SPD opposition hardens

On 26 May 1952 the Bonn treaty was concluded, and on 27 May the EDC treaty was signed in Paris. By this time it had become clear that the old SPD arguments centring around the lack of German 'Gleichberechtigung' and Germany's exposed strategic position, could no longer occupy the central place in the SPD campaign against the treaties. The great weakness in the argument that West Germany should not become the initial area of conflict was that in default of a common European defence organisation, it depended, as Schumacher recognised, on a much greater American commitment. It had by this time become apparent that the Americans were not prepared to make this commitment unless the West Germans made some contribution of their own. There was now a much greater emphasis, partly occasioned by the Soviet notes, on the harm that the treaties would do to German unity. Whereas before it had only been one of the objections and not always the most important one, it now became *the objection* to the treaties.

86

Schumacher, enjoying a last brief recovery, had written on 25 April, 'For we Social Democrats German unity takes priority over West European integration.'[65] In the Parliamentary Party Meeting of 21 May this new attitude is apparent. Baade, normally a moderate, wanted to use the term 'a second Versailles' to describe the treaties. Mommer proposed a 14-day strike by the Parliamentary Party and extra-parliamentary action. Brill, an even more fervent anti-communist than Schumacher, suggested direct negotiations with the Russians. These suggestions were not adopted, but the fact that they were made is symptomatic of the state of party opinion.

In an interview at the end of May, Schumacher used his most extreme language since his 'Chancellor of the Allies' taunt when he said that 'whoever agrees to this treaty stops being a German'. The signature of the treaties would be 'a completely crass victory celebration of the allied clerical coalition over the German people'.[66]

While the party took a more intransigent attitude towards the treaties at home it agreed in Strasbourg, in the Consultative Assembly of the Council of Europe on 30 May, to take part in the setting up of an ad hoc committee for the establishment of a European Political Authority. This step was taken partly on the Schumacher view that one must not pass up an opportunity to influence policy, partly because Schmid, a prominent figure in the delegation to the Council of Europe, had always been prominent in calling for such an authority.[67] However, after the EDC debates in July, the Parliamentary Party (on 15 July) refused to name any SPD representatives, and when the question was discussed at the opening session of the Common Assembly on 12 September 1952, it was attacked by Herbert Wehner.[68] At further meetings of the Council of Europe Assembly, on 16 January and 11 May 1953, it was attacked by SPD speakers.[69]

In June and early July the SPD's arguments against the treaties grew in volume and intensity. The same points cropped up in all the speeches. As the SPD objections grew in number and depth, the assertion in principle of agreement to a defence contribution diminished.

> No people can renounce its national unity and enter into a pact in which its delegations to other nations are to be more important than the liberty and coherence of its own population. National self-assertion is not the negation but rather the precondition of an endurable international co-operation.[70]

The ratification debates

The first reading took place on 9 July 1952. In his speech Dr Adenauer concentrated on making clear his own position, rather than criticising the SPD which had tabled a resolution calling on the government to press the Four Occupying Powers to begin talks on German unification as soon as possible. [71]

Carlo Schmid, the principal SPD speaker, based his arguments on the provisional nature of the Federal Republic and the dangers of integrating this rump Germany into a united Europe. In his speech, Schmid rejected very firmly the notion of neutrality, but added that the SPD's engagement for the West did not mean

> that one had to renounce the possibility of an independent German policy and follow a policy where attempts at power politics would be compensated with certainty by counter measures in the other part of Germany. [72]

It was not the case that there were only two alternatives, Eastern satellite or Western vassal. In his view there was a third:

> to ally oneself with the West in forms which the East did not need to find threatening and to enter into a relationship of free exchange with the East which strengthens the West instead of weakening it. [73]

Therefore the primary goal of German policy must be to bring about a four power conference.

Herbert Wehner introduced an SPD resolution on reunification. The question for him was not whether one could trust Soviet policy or not, but whether the policy of the Federal government was exploiting the chances of reunification or not. In Wehner's opinion the Chancellor calculated wrongly when he thought that West European integration would compel the Soviet government to accept German reunification. It was much more likely that the Soviet would reject it and even if one took an optimistic view of Soviet intentions, German reunification was thus tied in with so many other strategic and political factors as to render it impossible. Secondly, such a calculation rested on the assumption that the Western powers were in favour of German reunification — a very doubtful assumption, the more dangerous since Adenauer's method gave them a veto over German reunification. [74]

Fritz Erler, like Schmid and Wehner, dwelt on the immensity of the choice, either to attempt some relaxation of tension in the hope of promoting unity or to increase tension and diminish the prospects of unity by joining a competitive military alliance. [75]

After this first reading, the treaties were handed over to the specialist committees.

The death of Schumacher

Kurt Schumacher died on 22 August 1952. In many ways his death marks a watershed in the history of the post-war SPD. The changes which came, however, preceded his death. He had had his first stroke in October 1951, and the second, greater, stroke in January 1952 effectively ended his active involvement in politics. His style of 'opposition', which focussed on parliamentary duels with Adenauer, was an obvious first casualty. Ollenhauer was simply not credible as a parliamentary people's tribune. Opposition had spread, as we have seen, to the Constitutional Court. Later it was possible for Ollenhauer to embroil the trade unions and the Bundesrat in opposition to the EDC. This had proved very difficult up till then because Schumacher was unhappy with allies; he needed followers.

When Schumacher was in his prime he demanded from the party not only that all its members oppose Adenauer but that they do it for the same reasons as he did. This era now conclusively ended with his death. Where Schumacher relied on moral force, Ollenhauer put his money on tactics on winning elections. This view implied an orientation of his political actions to prevailing public opinion, an attitude which eventually led to the Bad Godesberg Programme. Ollenhauer, however, was also concerned about preserving the unity of the party and as the party's activists were generally less concerned than Ollenhauer and the Parliamentary Party about winning elections, their views acted as a significant check on the party leadership. Not surprisingly SPD policy, which although not free from contradictions had a certain grand clarity under Schumacher's autocratic leadership, became much more confused. To some extent this would have happened anyway, since the changed policy of the Soviet Union, and its attempt to seduce the Germans away from the EDC by offering them a chance of reunification, put the SPD in a very difficult position. Schumacher's virulent anti-communism rendered his commitment to German unity purely rhetorical. With the change in the Soviet attitude, the SPD was now put in a position where a failure to respond to Soviet advances would have exposed its policy for the rhetoric it was. Ollenhauer's response of increasing the rhetorical commitment to German unity, while stressing the necessity for free elections, was, though it rendered the proposals nugatory, probably the best that could be done.

At the same time as concentration on German unity, as the focus of opposition to the treaties, increased, arguments with an economic content started to diminish. This is partly, or even mainly, to be explained by the continuing prosperity. Schumacher's role is, however, not unimportant. Altough he was a life-long nationalist and therefore, in the SPD context, a revisionist, and though he technically understood little of economics, he remained until his death very much a socialist in economics. Accordingly, under Schumacher's leadership SPD opposition to European integration was pursued on the grounds of the harm it would do both to socialism in West Germany and German unity. Ollenhauer, aware of the unpopularity of socialist economics and confronted with ever growing prosperity, muted the arguments about the effects on the prospects of socialism within West Germany.

The Dortmund Party Conference

At the time of Schumacher's death the SPD opposition to the EDC, had two very different emphases, identified with Carlo Schmid and Gerhart Luetkens respectively. Carlo Schmid laid greater emphasis on substituting a system of collective security for integration into the Western Alliance and 'to bind the West together in a way that the East would not find threatening and treat with the East on the basis of free exchange which would strengthen the West rather than weakening it'. The other alternative, preserving the status quo and continuing with the Occupation Statute, continued to be identified with Dr Gerhart Luetkens.

There was also a tiny but very vocal group centred around Klaus Peter Schulz, that now declared its support for the treaties. Schulz was typical of this group in having easy access to the media, but no influence in the Party Executive. In two broadcasts in April, Schulz rejected the two extremes of neutrality and unilateral German rearmament. In Schulz's opinion the treaties fulfilled the preconditions advanced by the SPD in the February debate. The end result of the SPD's policy was sterility, since it had rejected equally neutralisation and rapprochement with the West. [76]

The differing conceptions of Schmid and Luetkens, already apparent in Parliamentary Party meetings, were publicly aired at the Dortmund Party Conference of 24–28 September, but nothing was heard from supporters of EDC like Schulz. Held in the shadow of Schumacher's death, it was a foregone conclusion that the Conference would confirm Ollenhauer as Party Chairman. The main interest of the Conference centred on the discussion of an 'Aktionsprogramm' which was intended to provide a clear framework for SPD opposition. The 'Aktionsprogramm' was also intended to make the SPD alternative clearer to the ordinary voter. Deputies had continually compained about confusion in the party faithful, because of the over-complicated nature of the opposition.

The opening speech was made by Ollenhauer. Typically for Ollenhauer,

90

the speech was entitled 'The unity of Germany and a viable Western Europe as the most urgent goal of SPD policy'. Schumacher would never have hedged his bets in a speech title. If the title faced both ways, the content was very much in the Schumacher mould. National unity was the paramount goal.

> Without the assurance of the national existence of our people, neither the construction of a viable Europe nor the realisation of democratic socialism is possible. [77]

Ollenhauer continued the Schumacher policy of placing full responsibility for reunification on the Four Occupying Powers. This had the great merit of absolving any West German government from dealing with the East German government since, despite its desire for negotiations with the USSR, the SPD remained as anti-communist as ever. [78]

Unlike at the Hamburg Conference, where Schumacher's speech gave rise to quite a bit of polemical discussion, Ollenhauer's speech provoked discussion which, while emanating from diffirent conceptions of Germany's position, was very largely agreed on the necessity of opposition to the EDC. The near unanimity of the Conference is to be explained by its nearness to the 1953 elections. The Conferences of 1950 and 1954 were much more polemical in tone than those of 1952 and 1956.

The 'Aktionsprogramm' adopted by the delegates on 28 September can best be described as generalities expressed in sharp tones. It was directed towards the long-term; there were none of the concrete measures demanded by Schumacher in his statement on 'opposition'. The main goal of the party was taken to be the preservation of peace.

On European issues generally, the programme was merely a summing up of what had already been said. The party ought to strive for the abolition of national sovereignties. Integration ought to be on the basis of equality. Such a Europe could not and should not be confined to the Six. The social aspects of integration were dwelt on in a critique of both the ECSC and EDC. In place of the EDC, the programme called for a system of collective security. [79]

The general result of the Dortmund Party Conference was an acceptance of the idea of a system of collective security hitherto identified with Carlo Schmid. This came paradoxically at a time when Schmid's influence in the Party was waning rapidly. [80] The notion of collective security was, however, not spelt out at all clearly at this time. It was not absolutely clear, for instance, whether the SPD leadership expected West Germany to make a military commitment to this system, or whether only a reunified Germany could participate in such a system. The idea of the programme had been to clarify issues for the ordinary voter — in this it had failed from the start.

The second reading, 3–5 December

This session had originally been scheduled to include the third reading as well. This was postponed because President Heuss had requested an advisory opinion on the treaties from the Federal Constitutional Court. The debate began with the reading of committee reports. The General Report was read by Willy Brandt in his capacity as Rapporteur of the Committee on the Occupation Statute and the Foreign Affairs Committee. The main thrust of Brandt's argument in the ensuing discussion was to reject the 'Junktim' between the lifting of the Occupation Statute and acceptance of EDC.[81]

Adenauer, under pressure from his own party, made acceptance of the treaties a matter of confidence, a question of 'the fate of Germany',[82] and castigated the SPD for its failure to produce a constructive alternative to alliance with the West.

Herbert Wehner, the SPD's principal speaker, claimed, in an attack on Adenauer, that the Western Allies, the USSR, and the Adenauer government were united in a tacit conspiracy to preserve the status quo and thereby the division of Germany.[83] On 4 December, Adenauer declared his intention to postpone the third reading until January, and to apply in the meantime for a ruling of the Constitutional Court that the treaties might be ratified by a simple majority of the Bundestag, since he was now convinced that he would not get a two-thirds majority. Ollenhauer led the SPD attack on the Chancellor, claiming that the decision to postpone the third reading and the appeal to the Court represented a real defeat for the government. He rejected Adenauer's contention that failure to ratify the EDC treaties would mean a return to the Occupation Statute: that instrument was dead; approval of the agreements meant approval of a status already out of date. Ollenhauer, after rejecting the EDC treaties declared that the SPD would be prepared to fight for democracy, without making it clear under what conditions they would contemplate such action. The basic thrust of his argument remained the danger to prospects of reunification presented by the treaties.[84]

The government got a fifty-vote majority on the treaties which could be taken as an SPD success. However the confused nature of the party's opposition to the EDC made it very unlikely that it would be able to capitalise on its success. The concept of 'collective security' officially

92

endorsed at Dortmund had made almost no appearance in the debate. Nearly all SPD members rejected the Western Alliance system, but there was almost no agreement on anything positive. [85]

In a press statement on 12 December 1952, Ollenhauer again declared that he supported a contribution by the Federal Republic to the defence of the free world.[86] This statement encouraged Adenauer to arrange a meeting between himself and Ollenhauer which took place on 18 December 1952. Adenauer stressed at this meeting that non-acceptance of the treaties would mean a reversion to the Occupation Statute and might also mean that the new Republican government in the United States would decide to concentrate on Asia. Ollenhauer maintained that the treaties were impregnated with distrust of Germany.[87] Ollenhauer then wrote a series of letters to Adenauer on 7, 16 and 22 January repeating the familiar charges of damage to reunification prospects, lack of 'Gleichberechtigung' and requested new elections. In his letter of 7 January Ollenhauer called for a system of collective security.[88]

That at least one prominent member of the SPD was thinking realistically at this time is evident in a memorandum by Herbert Wehner on SPD foreign policy. In this memorandum the two alternatives prepared by Carlo Schmid and Gerhart Luetkens were both dismissed. Schmid's concept of collective security was seen as being utopian, too dependent for its implementation on the great powers, offering Germany no leverage to exert influence. Luetkens' alternative was correctly seen as likely to isolate the SPD completely, both internally and externally. Wehner concluded that neither idea could be the basis of SPD action; what was needed was a scheme based on the fundamental premiss of tension between the USA and the USSR. [89]

The third reading

The third reading took place on 19 March 1953. This sitting took place just a fortnight after the death of Stalin on 5 March. Adenauer, in his opening speech, maintained that Stalin's death had provided the West with a valuable breathing space 'which hopefully would be useful to the European peoples in building up their defence'. Nothing would be more dangerous than to assume Stalin's death would usher in a period of detente. [90] He rejected absolutely the idea that it would be useful to negotitate with the Soviets before Western strength had been increased; 'there is no other way to German unity in freedom than to strengthen the West as much as possible'.[91]

93

Ollenhauer made perhaps the most important speech of his political career in rebutting Adenauer. In his view, the most important objection of the SPD to the EDC was its negative effect on the prospects of German unity. Adenauer's thesis of a 'policy of strength', which held that rearmament would make the Soviets readier to negotiate on the question of German unity, was very debatable. Similarly questionable was the assumption that the EDC treaties compelled the other signatories to accept German aspirations *vis-à-vis* reunification. It was likewise not the case that West Germany had become fully sovereign, since the so-called Emergency Clause reserved considerable rights of intervention to the Allies. 'Gleichberechtigung' was also denied to the West Germans, since their troops would be dependent for strategic and political guidance on the North Atlantic Council. While Ollenhauer rejected the view that the death of Stalin would mean a fundamental change in Soviet intentions, he held that there would, in all probability, be a change in tactics which would make negotiations more likely, but only if the EDC treaties were not signed. Ollenhauer, despite Wehner's advice, then proposed a system of collective security as an alternative. This security system would not be ruled by a supranational body (an *idée fixe* of Carlo Schmid's) but by a ministerial council. The participation of the Federal Republic in this organisation, whose relationship to NATO was still to be determined, was possible under the following preconditions:

1   Any treaty must leave the Federal Republic free to pursue the goal of German Unity.
2   This new Europe must be based on freedom and equality.
3   Such a system must guarantee the Federal Republic the same amount of security as the other partners.
4   It must include the United Kingdom, Denmark and Norway.
5   It must secure social welfare standards in the Federal Republic. [92]

Adenauer secured the ratification of the treaties by 224 votes to 166.

The Federal aspect

Thwarted in the Bundestag, blocked in the Federal Constitutional Court, and with the elections still six months off, the SPD seemed to have a chance of blocking the EDC in the Bundesrat. On this question no deviations were expected from the SPD mavericks in Bremen, Berlin and Hamburg. Kaisen, who was still as committed as ever to European unity,

94

had grave doubts about the wisdom of rearmament. [93] Willy Brandt had more or less stuck to the official line at Dortmund and in the ratification debates. Reuter, although continuing to appeal for a joint foreign policy, was very critical of Adenauer's neglect of the reunification issue. [94] Berlin in any case had no vote. Brauer had indicated in an interview with *Die Zeit* in March 1953 that, while he was much in favour of a European army on the Swiss model, he disapproved of the EDC. [95]

The opportunity for the SPD was created by the formation of an FDP/SPD coalition in Baden-Württemberg. This meant that if Baden-Württemberg, under Minister President Reinhold Maier, were to line up with the SPD the governing coalition could be outvoted 20–18 in the Bundesrat.

In the first sitting on 24 April, the most important speech was made by Wilhelm Kaisen. [96] Kaisen rejected the notion that it was a choice between East and West. The way to the East was blocked; neutrality would lead to isolation; identification with the West commanded general support. He supported the general foreign policy orientation of the government but had reservations about the EDC. Kaisen concluded that the EDC was demonstrably not in accordance with the Basic Law.

Despite Adenauer's personal intervention, Maier stuck to his negative resolution, which was adopted by 20 votes to 18. [97] This resolution asked for the Bundesrat to postpone its decision until the Federal Constitutional Court had ruled not only on the constitutionality of the treaties themselves, as demanded by the SPD, but also on the question of whether the Bundesrat was constitutionally empowered to approve only parts or all of the treaty complex.

Under great pressure from his own party, Maier finally agreed to accept a compromise solution, by which the Bundesrat would vote on the fiscal conventions of the EDC and on the status of Allied forces, but would not vote on the major treaties since the Basic Law did not specifically require ratification of treaties by the Bundesrat. In the debate of 15 May, which was chiefly notable for a strong speech by Brauer attacking the EDC, the treaties were adopted by 23 votes to 15. [98]

The DGB and rearmament

In the dispute over the EDC and in the 1953 election campaign, one of the SPD's strengths, in contradistinction to its experience in the battle against the Schuman Plan and the International Authority of the Ruhr, was the support of the DGB. The first position on rearmament taken by the DGB was in January 1950. The Executive Committee echoed conventional Western opposition to German remilitarisation by pointing out the dangers of revived militarism, the dangers of war by creating a *causus belli* between East and West, and the dangers of antagonising France without creating an effective bloc against threatened Soviet aggression. The DGB, however, added that remilitarisation under some circumstances might become possible, since Germany would want to contribute her share towards the defence of a united, free Europe aided by the US. [99]

With the outbreak of the Korean War, the Western attitude altered, and in November 1950, just after the DGB Executive had reasserted its conditional opposition to the revival of military forces, [100] the US High Commissioner appealed directly to labour leaders to support rearmament. By 1951 the DGB's attitude to rearmament had become less critical, for which there seem to be three main reasons: firstly, political pressure from the United States, to which it was very sensitive because of its awareness of the importance of the US in the economic field; secondly, following Böckler's death,, his replacement as Chairman by Christian Fette, who, though nominally an SPD member, had very bad relations with Schumacher; [101] thirdly, the hope for further concessions from Adenauer on co-determination.

The first opposition to the Executive line came at the Bavarian Regional Conference on 10 February 1952, when Fette and Hans vom Hoff were given a very rough handling. [102] On 28 and 29 February, the Executive had a special meeting with regional and local union officers. The Executive was over-ruled and the meeting endorsed the SPD position by calling for an immediate election to test public opinion. This was the first time that the position of the Executive had been seriously challenged. [103] At the second Congress of the DGB which met in Berlin in October 1952, Fette was replaced as Chairman by Walter Freitag, the Co-Chairman of I.G. Metall and SPD Deputy. In the discussion Fette requested that the DGB back the EDC but Freitag wanted to align the position of the DGB more with that of the SPD and it was Freitag's stand which was endorsed by the Conference. [104] Later, during the election campaign of 1953, the DGB was very much more identified with the SPD than had been the case in the first years, and it campaigned under the slogan of 'Choose a better Bundestag'.

The SPD campaign for the second Bundestag

The election campaign proper began with an Electoral Assembly, on

10 May at Frankfurt on Main, in which Ollenhauer concentrated on foreign policy. In his speech Ollenhauer repeated almost verbatim the speech he had made in the third ratification debate. There was, however, a difference of emphasis. It had then seemed that the European security system referred to by Ollenhauer was one which he envisaged the Federal Republic's being able to join. He now spoke of a 'system of collective security' which only a reunited Germany could join sometime in the future. [105] The confusion created was immense.

The SPD campaign was further weakened by the Bundesrat's acceptance of the EDC on 15 May. The Berlin uprising of 17 June was a further blow to SPD speakers, who had been stressing the possibility of relaxation of tension after Stalin's death. By the beginning of August, the CDU had swung over to the offensive and published four questions addressed to the SPD:

> 1   Does the SPD believe that Germany can be reunified without the co-operation of the democratic powers of the free world?
> 2   What other possibilities exist for co-operation with the West apart from the path chosen by the Federal government: i.e. the ECSC and the EDC?
> 3   Does the SPD believe that the Soviets can ever be impressed when Four Power conferences and reunification are being demanded without the Federal government first achieving the important international position which is being attained by the Federal government?
> 4   Is the SPD of the opinion that Germany should not continue to co-operate with either the Soviet Union or the Western powers? [106]

Ollenhauer refused to answer the questions, dismissing them as 'schoolmasterish'.

> The four questions of the CDU to the SPD became the main theme of the CDU election campaign in the foreign policy field, especially as the opposition of the SPD seemed all too complicated and full of imponderables in contrast to the simple, easily comprehensible government conceptions. [107]

The most important event of the SPD campaign was a press conference on 28 August at which Willi Eichler and Fritz Erler presented the party publication *Die Europapolitik der SPD*. Much of the publication is taken up with a condemnation of the ECSC. [108] As far as the EDC is concerned, it restricted itself to criticising the treaty without ever developing a defence conception of its own.

There is no mention of either branch of collective security, nor even an explicit statement of the Schumacher principle of the legitimacy of the defence of one's own country. More important for the campaign was Fritz Erler's statement at the press conference that the formation of an all-German government was a matter of great urgency, even when this meant that in one point it would not possess 'Handlungsfreiheit' — that is, it would not be free to bind itself to one or other of the military blocs. This caused immediate speculation in the West German press about an SPD change of attitude. [109] Ollenhauer took great pains, however, to re-establish the party position of no restrictions being placed on the treaty-making capacity of a future German government. [110]

In the event the combined effects of manifest American support, the obvious prosperity of the Federal Republic, the trauma of 17 June, and the popularity of European integration, ensured a handsome win for Adenauer. The CDU/CSU's percentage of votes cast rose from 31 to 45.2 per cent, while that of the SPD declined from 29.2 to 28.8 per cent. It was this defeat that really sparked off the long term process of change inside the SPD, not least in its attitude to European integration, and it is these changes that will be examined in the following pages.

The defeat of 6 September 1953 set off a long process of discussion and debate in the SPD not least in relation to rearmament. A first meeting of the Party Executive, Party Committee, Control Commission and Parliamentary Party was held on 17 September in Bonn. Ernst Reuter made one of his last important speeches and used the occasion to attack the Executive.

> Our organisation is not any worse than others. What is lacking is our intellectual ability to state clearly and unequivocally what we want in popular effective formulae. Our voters have understood what we do not want but we have seldom understood how to state clearly what we ourselves actually positively wanted; that is really the task which a great party, as is the case with the Social Democratic Party, has to solve ... the resolution which has been put to us is a petrifaction of this old-fashioned thinking, for it states what we are fighting against and what we are against. It does not state what the Social Democratic Party in this new Bundestag stands for. [111]

Reuter's appeal to the meeting on 17 September had little success. The resolution which maintained that the SPD campaign policy had been correct was adopted by an overwhelming majority. This resolution specified three goals for the SPD:

1   The absolute primacy of reunification.

2 The integration of a free and democratic Germany into a community of free peoples on the basis of equality.

3 The establishment of a better democratic and social order in Germany.

The meeting of 17 September did not, however, put an end to discussion in the party. One set of proposals which attracted wide publicity at the time was produced by a group of Berlin students. Entitled 'Fifteen theses for the renewal of the SPD', thesis 9, which was specifically concerned with foreign policy stated:

> The foreign policy of the party up to now has met with a lack of comprehension among the voters. In questions of foreign policy we should look more for the points which we have in common with the Government than those which distinguish us from it. A united foreign policy of all democratic parties would be of great advantage ... We propose a European union ... All this does not, however, mean that we should renounce the decisive factors of our Socialist foreign policy (reunification of Germany, prevention of a new militarism, 'Gleichberechtigung' for our people within the framework of the free nations of Europe and the world) for reasons of opportunism. [113]

The Party Executive at first made no response to this discussion, but some three months later it did institute two commissions to direct discussion in the party. Not surprisingly, this discussion largely served to strengthen the conviction in the minds of executive members that they had been right all along. [114]

The SPD was heartened by the decision of the three Western powers at their Washington Conference to ask the Soviet Union to a Four Power conference in 1954. This was eventually fixed for January/February 1954. At the meeting of the Party Executive on 11–12 December 1953, a resolution was adopted welcoming the Four Power talks and appealing to the Four Powers to explore every avenue which might lead to understanding. [115]

The Conference held in Berlin failed to reach any sort of agreement despite the efforts of British Foreign Secretary, Anthony Eden. The SPD, however, did not take this to be a signal for the revision of its policy – rather the reverse – and this despite the fact that it had maintained since Dortmund that it would be prepared to make a military contribution if it became apparent that the Soviet Union was not interested in reunification and collective security. In a communiqué issued after a meeting of the leading party organs on 20 February 1954, the party regretted the outcome of the conference and appealed to the Four Powers to permit German reunification on the basis of free elections and also to allow the reunified Germany to participate in a viable system of collective security. [116]

There was, however, some opposition to the leadership policy inside the party. On 25 February Karl Schiller published an article in *Die Welt*, where he argued:

> One must consider very seriously whether a policy of negation is today still in keeping with our times and whether it can be maintained. The old SPD demand for Big Four talks before integration has been fulfilled, and after this test has turned out to be negative, this should now be reason enough for the SPD — quite in keeping with its former political line — to turn attention positively to the question of European integration.

Schiller claimed that it was becoming more and more obvious that the leadership contemplated collective security only after reunification — a departure in his view from the sense of the Dortmund programme.

> If in the new situation the policy of saying No brought us reunification or even only one step nearer to it, one would have to support it without any reservations. It now leads, however — unfortunately Berlin has demonstrated that — along the endless road of Moscow delays, with a No to the common strengthening of Europe and the Free World. Now, after the Berlin Conference, the SPD has lost an important bargaining point, without thereby being able, however, to do something for reunification.

Similar sentiments were expressed by Klaus-Peter Schulz in *Sorge um die deutsche Linke*. [117] During Schumacher's active political life, Schulz had been fairly close to the leadership and had edited an official party publication, *Vor der schwersten Entscheidung* on rearmament. In contrast, *Sorge um die deutche Linke* is predominantly critical in tone, since 'an opposition policy which, despite all its dubiousness, had had line and contours under Schumacher's directives, has now completely deteriorated into a vague state of permanent, uncreative small-mindedness.'[118] Schulz pointed out the contradiction involved in demanding simultaneously reunification and 'Gleichberechtigung', since reunification implied the provisional nature of West Germany which would mean that the real 'Gleichberechtigung' would be impossible. [119] In Germany's position, Schulz claimed, reunification could not be made the basis of a viable political programme as had been attempted by the SPD: it could only represent a long-term goal. [120]

At this point Kaisen, Brauer and, more surprisingly, Erwin Schoettle, revised their earlier views and called for a change in the party's European policy and at least limited support for German participation in the EDC. [121]

In the Bundestag debate on 25–26 February 1954, the party leadership went some way to meet these objectives. After Ollenhauer had reasserted the SPD's opposition to the EDC, he added that rejection of the EDC did not mean rejection of a policy of military security for Germany. [122] 'Our No to this monster includes a Yes to the creation of a sensible democratic concept of defence.' [123] This was an almost perfect illustration of what Schulz meant when he wrote:

> If one berated it for its eternal negative standpoint, whether out of malice or honest concern, it reacted with irritation or embitterment with the argument that it had never said No, but that each No was to be seen as a Yes with conditions. [124]

At the first meeting of the Security Committee on 8 May 1954, and at its third on 19 June 1954, great concern was expressed at the lack of clarity in party policy. [125] At the first meeting Helmut Schmidt, the youngest member of the SPD Parliamentary Party, complained:

> The people expect the SPD to state its position with regard to the military question. H. Bombs – Yes or No? Defence – Yes or No? Apparently we are not yet in agreement on the central issue. [126]

The Berlin Conference

In the weeks before the party's Berlin Conference, the press reported on the resolutions sent in by local party organisations and predicted a very stormy conference. Ollenhauer, in an interview on 9 July 1954, aware of the pressure being put on Mendes-France by the United States and fairly sure of the EDC's failure, declared that the SPD would refuse to accept a solution of Germany's security problem which did not include France or was directed against her. [127] This theme was to reappear during the Party Conference. It was essentially a tactical move on the part of the SPD, since it offered it a chance of attacking Adenauer's exposed flank: his complete attachment to Franco–German friendship.

The key speech at the Conference was made by Ollenhauer and called for the creation of a European security system. However, he did not exclude the possibility of rearmament before reunification, [128] a view also taken by Fritz Erler. Fritz Erler had by this time begun the gradual *volte-face* that was to turn him by the late fifties into one of NATO's most enthusiastic supporters. He contested the view that West Germany should do nothing about defence until reunification had been achieved adding 'Whoever does not want the EDC must put something else, something better in its place. I am not speaking now of the military, I am speaking of the political aspect of this question.'[129] On the general question of European integration, Erler said that the SPD must indicate much more clearly than hitherto how it was going to work for European unity. It must get beyond an empty verbal commitment.

Most of the speeches from the floor were, however, critical of the party leadership, and the reception accorded to the last speaker, Max Kunze, who had attacked the Party Executive in the name of the local activists, made explicit the pacifist feelings which motivated many of the delegates. [130]

The Party Executive was not a little embarrassed by the attacks from the floor. In his closing speech, Ollenhauer regretted that, in the exhaustive debate, one point had gained undue prominence. He then reiterated the party's rejection of the EDC and the continued primacy of reunification — a primacy which demanded the reopening of Four Power negotiations. [131]

The main resolution opposed to the Party Executive resolution was Article 113, which asked for a complete rejection of rearmament. It was rejected by an overwhelming majority. [132] After some rewriting, the Party Executive resolution was then adopted. Some alterations, minor in scope, were made to the Dortmund programme. [133] A more reliable indication of the delegates' mood is provided by the elections to the Executive. Fritz Wenzel, Heinz Kühn and Willi Birkelbach, all prominent opponents of rearmament, were elected, while Erler and Brandt failed to be elected.

Superficially then, there was nothing terribly novel in the result of the Berlin Conference. It did, however, show Ollenhauer how strong the pacifist currents were among party members. Ollenhauer, a lifelong apparatchik, was rarely willing to go faster than the mass of the party members. After the Conference no-one doubted that the party would continue to oppose the EDC or a successor organisation, and that it would reject bipartisanship in foreign policy. What was open to doubt was how far the leadership would go to meet some of the more extreme party members.

The first important statement on defence after the Berlin Conference was made by Ollenhauer at a press conference in Bonn on 24 August 1954. [134] Ollenhauer called for a bipartisan foreign policy focussed on the reunification issue. Most of the answers he gave were conventional, even platitudinous, but the weakness of the party's position was exposed when he was unable to furnish a clear answer to what the attitude of the SPD would be if West Germany were offered 'Gleichberechtigung' in NATO.

The end of the EDC

The EDC treaty was in fact rejected on 31 August 1954 by the French National Assembly. It appeared even to Adenauer that his policy had run into a cul-de-sac. However, a quick patching-up operation was carried out at Eden's prompting, and a conference was arranged for 28 September to 3 October in London.

The first official SPD reaction was contained in a leading article in *Neuer Vorwärts* entitled 'End of the EDC turning point in policy'. Gerhart Gleissberg, the editor, a man on the left of the SPD, condemned any attempts to set up an 'Ersatz-EDC'. Now was the time to call another Four Power conference. [135]

By the time Ollenhauer spoke again, Eden had resuscitated the corpse of a Western European defence organisation. In a speech to the Parliamentary Party on 22 September 1954, Ollenhauer made his position clear: the hesitancy of 24 August had been replaced by definite opposition.

> I will only say one thing, that, if the present period of negotiations ends with German entry into NATO, then the possibility of unity is, for all practical purposes, dead. We therefore have to oppose here the whole question, being handled under only the narrow aspect of a substitute security system for the EDC. [136]

These developments were first debated in the Bundestag on 7 October. Ollenhauer took the principle role in the SPD attack on the government. He claimed with some justification that the London agreements represented a departure from previous government policy, that:

> The form of the co-operation which was agreed upon in London, with complete renunciation of the supranational integrative character of the EDC, corresponds more to Social Democratic views than to the policy of integration held by of the majority in this House till now. [137]

The London agreements were therefore an advance on the EDC in at least two respects: namely British participation, and their non-supranational character. Despite these improvements, defects remained, and Ollen-

103

hauer stressed the importance of social rather than military security. This point, which carried a lot of force in 1950, was beginning to look a bit threadbare in the prosperous Germany of 1954. He concluded by repeating the by now familiar demands for Four Power talks and the creation of a European collective security system.

An important speech was made by Adolf Arndt who introduced the concept of 'Bündnisfreiheit' (Freedom from Alliances) in his speech. This concept of 'Bündnisfreiheit' or 'Bündnislösigkeit', really indistinguishable from a neutralist position, was to figure ever more prominently in SPD speeches in the coming months. [138]

The SPD position of opposition to the new developments was strengthened by the outcome of the third DGB Congress of 4–9 October in Frankfurt, where the delegates endorsed a motion expressing disapproval of the creation of a national army as envisaged at the London Conference. [139] A meeting of the leading organs of the party on 16 October 1954 endorsed the stand of the Parliamentary Party and repeated the Parliamentary Party's demands in a resolution. [140] Further meetings took place between the Western powers in Paris on 19–23 October. At the close of these meetings the so-called Paris Accords were concluded. These inter-alia ended the occupation regime in the Federal Republic, integrated West Germany into the Western Alliance system, via a restyled Brussels Pact, and attempted to map out a solution of the Saar issue. In his speech to the Parlimentary Party on 20 November 1954, Ollenhauer, although still prepared to concede some advances in WEU as against EDC, rejected German membership because of the dangers to German unity. Ollenhauer's rejection of the Paris Accords was confirmed in the Party Executive resolution of 6 November. [141]

The first reading of the WEU (Western European Union) treaty took place in the Bundestag on 15–16 December. In the Budesrat debate on 10 December, Kaisen, as Rapporteur of the Foreign Affairs Committee, had in general spoken in favour of the Accords, except for that Accord dealing with the Saar. The first three Accords were adopted against the votes of Hesse and Lower Saxony, with Bremen abstaining on the Accord dealing with German participation in NATO. The Bundesrat reserved its opinion on the Saar Accord. [142]

The SPD had advanced a complex of resolutions for the Bundestag debate of 15 December, dealing with reunification, the London Agreements, Four Power negotiations and the Saar. Erich Ollenhauer repeated the familiar arguments, stressing that the Soviet note of 9 November offered some possibility of negotiation. [143]

Fritz Erler was given the more difficult task of rejecting the government charge of inconsistency. While it was true that the SPD had opposed EDC *inter-alia* because it did not give West Germany direct entry into NATO, this argument was now redundant. The main objection was 'that the Federal Republic is being absorbed in a military alliance system as if there were no other Germany'. 'That is the main objection.'[144] The FDP joined the SPD in opposing the agreement on the Saar.

In the last months of 1954 and early 1955, the SPD opposition became shriller than hitherto. Phrases like 'Nationales Unglück' (national misfortune) and 'Ermächtigungsgesetz' (enabling act) were used to describe the treaties. The Soviet Note of 15 January led to renewed demands for negotiation.[145] Demands for a general strike against rearmament were current among the trade union rank and file, and less ambitious proposals by Bavarian trade unionists, to hold plebiscites in all West German Länder, conduct a secret vote among union membership and grant legal protection to trade unionists who refused military service, were endorsed by other regional leaders if not by the DGB Executive Committee.[146]

The Paulskirche movement

Co-operation between the trade unions and the SPD reached a new level of intimacy in the Paulskirche movement. At a meeting held on 29 January 1955 in the historic Paulskirche in Frankfurt, Erich Ollenhauer for the SPD, George Reuter for the DGB, Gustav Heinemann and assorted notables launched a 'German manifesto' calling for an end to military integration with the West because of the damage it would do to German unity. Couched in the language of the 'ohne mich' movement, it warned against a situation in which German would have to shoot on German.

There is, I think, some evidence that the DGB were less whole-heartedly behind the movement than the SPD. Freitag did not sponsor the manifesto and there were others who had reservations. Reuter stressed that he spoke as an individual. The SPD leadership, outwardly at least, appeared more enthusiastic, since it was under pressure not only from the rank and file but Wenzel, Kühn and Birkelbach in the Party Executive. That some of this enthusiasm was feigned is clear, and there is a lot of justice in Pirker's observations:

> The convocation of a protest meeting in the Paulskirche as the prelude to a popular movement against the treaties presented an open attack against the anti-plebiscitarian elements laid down in the constitution by the SPD itself. The Paulskirche action had fundamentally, how-

ever, the object of drawing off the increasing radicalism into legitimate avenues. It was conceived of as an emotional and verbal protest against Adenauer's policy, as a safety valve for the pressure within the party and the trade unions, and nothing more.[147]

There was some articulate opposition to the Paulskirche movement inside the SPD. Herbert Wehner, as an ex-communist with great experience in demonstrations, warned against the dangers of putting too much reliance on mass-action.

> For this reason I queried then how things would develop if one were to come to a point where the parliamentary opposition were exhausted and no longer capable of increased efforts, whether one wanted with all ensuing consequences to take to the streets or not. Since I presumed that no-one wanted that, and, since I myself saw no possibility, even if one wanted to, of achieving in this way anything which could prove of use for our people, I considered these actions to be dangerous. I considered it dangerous to arouse moods, to gather people with whom Social Democracy, from a specific point onwards, could not progress any further, and in addition *thereby destroy the way to the so-called average man.* [148]

The SPD sponsored demonstrations in Dortmund, Hamburg, Herford, Hof and Aschaffenburg. On 17 February the DGB published a resolution urging suspension of ratification until new high-level Four Power talks were held and warning of the unfavourable domestic consequences of remilitarisation.[149] Spontaneous demonstrations of massive proportions occurred in Frankfurt and Munich. The SPD leadership was in something of a cleft stick. It had always rejected plebiscites and extra-parliamentary action in the past, but it now espoused it because of the seriousness of the situation. It remained, however, convinced of parliamentary democracy, and took part in the parades with some embarrassment. While 'the party progressed with these actions along the brink of the constitution, it was, however, only on the brink, for it was only all too aware of the anti-plebiscitarian boundaries of the Basic Law'. [150]

The demonstrations proved to have little effect on the Bundestag (it could arguably be said to have strengthened the government). The arguments on ending the Occupation Statute, on the stationing of foreign troops in West Germany, and on the accession of West Germany to the Brussels and NATO pacts all received, on 24–27 February, a majority of over 150 votes. The Saar agreement, which might have made it possible, had the SPD pursued a different tactic, to win over the FDP was passed by only 61 votes. Such a defeat for the SPD justifies Pirker's epitaph, 'Die Bewegung von historischer Bedeutung war politisch verpufft'. (The movement of historical importance fell flat politically.)

On 18 March the Bundesrat ratified all the Agreements without opposition. On 4 May the Constitutional Court, which had been asked by the SPD to declare the Saar Agreement unconstitutional, found that the Basic Law had not been broken. On 5 May 1955 the agreements came into force.

SPD opposition to rearmament continued in one form or another till 1958, but after the signing of WEU treaty, defence and European policy were no longer bound together. This development, more than any other factor, made possible the party's change of course on European integration. Until then the salience of the defence question, unpopular with both the electorate and the SPD rank and file, prevented even an appearance of bipartisanship in foreign policy and support of the government's policy of West European integration. Now that the question of integration was separated from defence, it was possible for the SPD leadership to support integration. The failure of the Paulskirche movement was crucial to this development, since its manifest failure discredited the militants who had been strengthened by the Berlin Conference. It was this that made possible the view, later to be identified with Wehner, that SPD influence was heightened by collaboration with, rather than opposition to, the government.

Notes

[1] For a general overview of this extraordinarily complex issue, see M. Dormann, *Demokratische Militärpolitik, die Alliierte Militär strategie als Thema deutscher Politik 1948 – 68*, Freiburg 1970. A much more incisive, though less detailed, view is provided by J. Richardson, *Germany and the Atlantic Alliance – the Interaction of Strategy and Politics*, Harvard 1966. On the SPD see especially Udo Löwke, *Für den Fall dass, SPD und Wehrfrage 1949–55*, Hanover 1970.

[2] J. Richardson, *Germany and the Atlantic Alliance – The Interaction of Strategy and Politics*, Harvard 1966, p. 17.

[3] *L'Est Republicain* 14 December 1949. Filed in SPD Archive under J. 37 (debate on rearmement)

[4] *FAZ*, 5 December 1949; K. Adenauer, op. cit., vol. 1 pp. 267–8.

[5] K. Adenauer, op. cit., p. 268.

[6] Cited in G. Wettig, *Entmilitarisierung und Wiederbewaffnung in*

Deutschland 1943–55. Internationale Auseinandersetzungen um die Rolle der Deutschen in Europa, Munich 1967, p. 304.

[7] Deutscher Bundestag, *Verhandlungen* 16 December 1949, pp. 734–5 (K. Adenauer); ibid., pp. 735ff. (E. Ollenhauer); SPD, *Jahrbuch 1948–49*, pp. 23ff.

[8] *FAZ*, 26 July 1950.

[9] *Sopade* no. 901, August 1950, pp. 7–9.

[10] Ibid., p. 79.

[11] Ibid., pp. 80–3.

[12] *The Times*, 12 August 1950.

[13] Reprinted by the Party Executive as 'Die Deutsche Sicherheit – Die Sozialdemokratie zur Verteidigung Deutschlands', Bonn 1950.

[14] Ibid., p. 8.

[15] Ibid., p. 11.

[16] *The Times*, 31 August 1950.

[17] *The Times*, 3 September 1950.

[18] *Sopade* no. 902, pp. 1–14.

[19] J. Richardson, op. cit., pp. 1–24, for the most perspicacious account of Allied diplomacy on this question at the time.

[20] Talk on Bavarian Radio on 28 October, in Frankfurt on 29 October (*FAZ* 30 October 1950), and to the Parliamentary Party on 1 November (Sopade no. 903, pp. 4–9).

[21] *Protokoll der Fraktionssitzung* 20 October 1950. On Niemöller see very important new work: Dieter Koch, *Heinemann und die Deutschland Frage*, Munich 1972.

[22] *Protokoll der Fraktionssitzung* 1 November 1950. Speech reprinted by SPD Executive as 'Das Volk soll Entscheiden' in *Sopade* no. 903, pp. 4–9. He had mentioned the question of new elections on 24 October 1950 (see *FAZ* 25 October 1950).

[23] *Protokoll der Fraktionssitzung* 1 November 1950.

[24] Ibid.

[25] *Sopade* no. 903, p. 9.

[26] *Sopade* no. 904, December 1950, pp. 3–5. Report of speech by K. Adenauer.

[27] *Sopade* no. 904, December 1950, pp. 5–7. Report of speech by K. Schumacher.

[28] *Bremer Nachrichten* 30 January 1951.

[29] *FAZ* 9 June 1951.

[30] *Die Tat*, Zurich 27 May 1951.

[31] Deutscher Bundestag, *Verhandlungen*, 16 October 1951, p. 6929 (G. Luetkens).

[32] Ibid., p. 6945 (E. Ollenhauer).

[33] Filed under J.37 (debate on rearmament).

[34] Deutscher Bundestag, *Verhandlungen* 9 January 1952, pp. 7595–60 (K. Adenauer).

[35] Deutscher Bundestag, *Verhandlungen*, 16 January 1952, pp. 7855–6 (E. Ollenhauer).

[36] *Die Welt*, 22 January 1952.

[37] *Protokoll der Fraktionssitzung*, 15 January 1952.

[38] In my account I rely heavily on Karl Loewenstein.'The Bonn Constitution and the European Defense Community treaties – a study in judicial frustration' *Yale Law Journal*, 1955, pp.806–39. This is a staggeringly brilliant piece of judicial compression. The accounts in other works like Baring, and Wettig are but pale shadows of this essay.

[39] Loewenstein, op. cit., p. 809.

[40] Judgment of Bundesverfassungsgericht (I Senat), 30 July 1952, IBVG 396 I Wehrbeitrag 436.

[41] Loewenstein, op. cit., pp. 861–7.

[42] Bonn treaty, Article 73.

[43] These issues are treated in Löwenstein, op. cit., pp. 817–27.

[44] *Protokoll der Fraktionssitzung*, 5 February 1952.

[45] Ibid.

[46] Deutscher Bundestag, *Verhandlungen*, 7 February 1952, pp. 8095–108 (K. Adenauer).

[47] Ibid., pp. 8108–16. On address to party meeting see 'Zur Debatte um den Wehrbeitrag' (J.37, debate on rearmament, Nachlass E. Ollenhauer).

[48] Ibid., p. 1, section 1C: 'The Saar Question – particular care will be required since, as I warned two weeks ago, Adenauer is likely to score a success in this area.'

[49] Deutscher Bundestag, *Verhandlungen*, 7 February 1952, pp. 8183–96 (C. Schmid).

[50] Ibid., pp. 8234–9 (E. Ollenhauer). All the SPD speeches were reprinted as *Sozialdemokratie und Wehrbeitrag*, issued by the Party Executive, 1952

[51] 'Sozialdemokratie und Wehrbeitrag', 2nd part, pp. 21–3, gives details of voting.

[52] *Protokoll der Fraktionssitzung*, 12 February 1952.

[53] Text filed under Q7.

[54] Cited J. Richardson, op. cit., p. 25.

[55] K. Adenauer, *Erinnerungen* vol. 2 (1953–55) pp. 80–9.

[56] *Sopade* no. 920, pp. 9–10.

[57] For above see *Protokoll der Fraktionsitzung*, 11 March 1952.

[58] *Sopade* no. 920, p. 9.

[59] Ibid.

[60] J. Richardson, op. cit., p. 25.

[61] *Protokoll der Fraktionssitzung*, 22 April 1952.

[62] F. Erler, *Democracy in Germany*, Harvard 1965, p. 49.

[63] P. Windsor, *City on Leave*, 1963, pp. 187—8.

[64] *Sopade* no. 921, pp. 4—6.

[65] *Neuer Vorwärts*, 25 April 1952, p. 1.

[66] *Sopade* no. 922, June 1952, pp. 3—4.

[67] Proceedings of the Council of Europe Consultative Assembly, 30 May 1952, pp. 231ff (K. Mommer), pp. 267ff (C. Schmid).

[68] Proceedings of the ECSC, Common Assembly, 12 September 1952, p. 84 (H. Wehner) *French edition*.

[69] Proceedings of the Council of Europe Consultative Assembly, 16 January 1953 p. 90ff. (F. Erler) 11 May 1953, p. 149ff.

[70] K. Schumacher, 12 June 1952, cited in U.F. Löwke *Für den Fall dass, SPD und Wehrfrage 1949—55*, Hanover 1969, p. 106.

[71] For .SPD resolution see R11A (Documents 1952) p. 178, and for Adenauer Deutscher Bundestag *Verhandlungen* 9 July 1952, pp. 9789—801 (K. Adenauer).

[72] Deutscher Bundestag, *Verhandlungen*, 9 July 1952, p.9817 (C. Schmid).

[73] Ibid.

[74] Deutscher Bundestag, *Verhandlungen*, 10 July 1952, pp. 9871—76 (H. Wehner).

[75] Ibid., pp. 9902—7 (F. Erler).

[76] K.P. Schulz 'Probleme der Zeit' S.W. Funk, 21 April 1952; 'Die Rolle der SPD in der Aussenpolitik' S.W. Funk, 28 April 1952.

[77] *Protokoll des Dortmunder Parteitages der SPD*, p. 33.

[78] The whole text of the speech is to be found in *Protokoll des Dortmunder Parteitages*, pp. 33—50.

[79] *Aktionsprogramm der SPD beschlossen auf dem Dortmunder Parteitag 28 September 1952,*, SPD Party Executive, October 1952, *passim.* Reproduced O. Flechtheim, *Dokumente zur parteipolitischen Entwicklung in Deutschland seit 1945*, vol. 3, pp. 64—86.

[80] See anonymous report that I discovered among the Erler papers, which were at that time (1969) unsorted. Reproduced in full in my Ph.D. thesis, p. 165.

[81] Deutscher Bundestag, *Verhandlungen*, 3 December 1952, pp. 11,111—16 (W. Brandt).

[82] Ibid., pp. 11,132–44 (K. Adenauer). Citation p. 11,144.

[83] Ibid., pp. 11,116–19 (H. Wehner).

[84] Deutscher Bundestag, *Verhandlungen*, 5 December 1952, pp. 11,445–62 (E. Ollenhauer).

[85] See U. Löwke, op. cit., pp. 139–40.

[86] *Neuer Vorwärts*, 19 December 1952.

[87] *Die Welt*, 19 December 1952.

[88] See Nachlass Ollenhauer, speeches and articles 1952, 61; Adenauer *Erinnerungen* vol. 2, pp. 188ff.

[89] No date is given. Filed under J.34 (Nachlass Ollenhauer, foreign policy 1951–55).

[90] Deutscher Bundestag, *Verhandlungen*, 17 March 1953, pp. 12,300–11 (K. Adenauer). Citation p. 12,302.

[91] Deutscher Bundestag, *Verhandlungen*, 19 March 1953 (K. Adenauer). Citation p. 12,306.

[92] Ibid., pp. 12,317–28 (E. Ollenhauer).

[93] His criticism of Schumacher, in relation to rearmament, had been directed more at the tone than the context of Schumacher's policy. Indeed, in conversation with me, he continually condemned Schumacher as being too Prussian, too militaristic. There had also been a meeting on 22 February 1953, between Bremen SPD members and Ollenhauer, at which Kaisen was present and an agreement on EDC was reached (*Weser Kurier*, Bremen, 23 February 1953). Moreover, on 15 April 1953 the Bremen Bürgerschaft had passed a strong motion condemning the EDC (Bremer Bürgerschaft *Steno Berichte*, 15 April 1953, p. 214).

[94] See Brandt and Löwenthal, op. cit., p. 640.

[95] *Die Zeit*, 19 March 1953.

[96] Deutscher Bundesrat, *Verhandlungen*, 24 April 1953, pp. 183–5 (W. Kaisen).

[97] Ibid., pp. 186–8 (K. Adenauer). Adoption 191. Resolution: Br. Drucks, 166/53 C and D.

[98] Deutscher Bundesrat, *Verhandlungen*, 15 May 1953, pp. 234–5 (M. Brauer). This episode is described in A. Baring, 'Aussenpolitik in Adenauer's Kanzlerdemokratie' and A.J. Heidenheimer, 'Federalism and the party system', *American Political Science Review (ASPR)*, 1959, pp. 809–28.

[99] Cited in G. Braunthal, 'West German trade unions and disarmament', *Political Science Quarterly*, 1958, p. 84.

[100] DGB *News Letter*, 25 November 1950.

[101] These bad relations were partly caused by Schumacher's inability to see the relationship in anything other than Weimar terms. Anna-Maria

Renger, when talking about this period to me spoke of 'disloyalty' on the part of Fette. These judgements are based on my interview with vom Hoff.

[102]   *Welt der Arbeit*, 19 February 1952.

[103]   *Welt der Arbeit*, 7 March 1952.

[104]   DGB, *Protokoll Ordentlicher Bundeskongress Berlin* (13–17 October 1952), pp. 115–6, pp. 168–9.

[105]   *Die Welt*, 11 May 1953.

[106]   Hirsch Weber and Schutz, *Wähler und Gewählte*, Berlin 1957, p. 121–2.

[107]   Ibid., p. 122.

[108]   *Die Europapolitik der SPD*. SPD Party Executive, Bonn 1953, pp. 21ff.

[109]   See H. Bretton 'The German Social Democratic Party and the international situation' *APSR*, December 1953, pp. 980–96 (esp. pp. 993–4).

[110]   *FAZ*, 4 September 1953.

[111]   Brandt and Löwenthal *Ernst Reuter*, op. cit., p. 700. Reuter continued his attack on the Party Executive at a meeting of Berlin Party Functionaries where he made an appeal for an unequivocal SPD attitude towards the defence question (ibid, p. 702).

[112]   Löwke, op. cit., p. 160.

[113]   Filed in library of SPD Party Executive under J.33 (Foreign policy after 1945).

[114]   Löwke, op. cit., p. 161.

[115]   *FAZ*, 13 December 1954.

[116]   *FAZ*, 21 February 1954.

[117]   K.P. Schulz, *Sorge um die deutsche Linke*, Cologne 1954.

[118]   Ibid., p. 58.

[119]   Ibid., p. 59.

[120]   Ibid., p. 64.

[121]   M. Burg, 'Nicht in allen Teilen Wasserdicht – Die SPD Politik während der Berliner Konferenz' *Rheinischer Merkur*, 26 February 1954.

[122]   Deutscher Bundestag, *Verhandlungen*, 25 February 1954, p. 527 (E. Ollenhauer).

[123]   Deutscher Bundestag, *Verhandlungen*, 26 February 1954, p. 564 (E. Ollenhauer).

[124]   K. Schulz, op. cit., p. 54.

[125]   Protocols of this Committee can be found in the Nachlass Ollenhauer.

[126]   Nachlass Ollenhauer.

[127]   For press reports indicating a stormy conference see *Die Freiheit*

Mainz, 30 June 1954, 'Das Parteibarometer der SPD steht auf Sturm' *Die Welt*, Essen. For Ollenhauer's interview see *FAZ*, 10 July 1954.

[128]   *Protokoll des Parteitages der SPD*, Berlin 1954, pp. 54–7.

[129]   Ibid., pp. 79–80 (F. Erler).

[130]   Ibid., pp. 140–2 (M. Kunze).

[131]   Ibid., pp. 145–6 (E. Ollenhauer).

[132]   Ibid., p. 148.

[133]   Unfavourable references to the ECSC were excised; see Flechtheim, op. cit., pp. 96–9.

[134]   *FAZ*, 25 August 1954.

[135]   *Neuer Vorwärts*, 3 September 1954.

[136]   *Protokoll der Sitzung der SPD Bundestagsfraktion*, 22 September 1954.

[137]   Deutscher Bundestag, *Verhandlungen*, 7 October 1954, p. 2335 (E. Ollenhauer).

[138]   Ibid., p. 2303 (A. Arndt).

[139]   *FAZ*, 10 October 1954.

[140]   *FAZ*, 18 October 1954.

[141]   The text of this resolution and Ollenhauer's speech to the Parliamentary Party is to be found in the Nachlass Ollenhauer (Speeches, essays and press conference, July–December 1954).

[142]   Deutscher Bundestag, *Verhandlungen*, 1C December 1954, pp. 368–71.

[143]   Deutscher Bundestag, *Verhandlungen*, 15 December 1954, pp. 3135–7 (E. Ollenhauer).

[144]   Deutscher Bundestag, *Verhandlungen*, 16 December 1954, p. 3204 (F. Erler).

[145]   Löwke, op. cit., p. 207.

[146]   G. Braunthal, 'West Germany trade unions and disarmament' *Political Science Quarterly*, 1958, p. 91.

[147]   Pirker, op. cit., p. 205.

[148]   See G. Gaus, *Staatserhaltende Opposition oder hat die SPD kapitüliert?* Hamburg 1966, p. 26.

[149]   *FAZ*, 18 February 1955.

[150]   Pirker, op. cit., p. 209.

[151]   Pirker, op. cit., p. 205.

5　EEC and Euratom –
the SPD Changes Course

The entry of the SPD into Jean Monnet's Action Committee for the United States of Europe is the outward and visible sign of a real change in the party's attitude. This particular phase of SPD policy is, surprisingly, the least researched: the dramatic figure of Schumacher and his clear cut policies have proved much more attractive than the rather two-dimensional figure of Ollenhauer.[1]

It was the separation of the issues of defence and European integration brought about by West German entry into NATO which made this change possible. We have already seen in Chapter 4 how difficult it was to get the party to change its policy on defence. This does not of itself provide sufficient answer as to why the SPD changed course. Like most historical events and processes this change resists a mono-casual explanation. Among the other important factors were the attitude of the trade unions, the relaxation of tension over the Saar, the SPD experience in the European Assemblies, the failure of the SPD's previous policy, movement inside the party, the Messina Conference and the Monnet Committee.

Attitude of the trade unions

One of the most striking characteristics of the SPD in the post-Schumacher era was its very close co-operation with the DGB. This phase lasted until the removal of Walter Freitag from his post as Chairman in 1956. The DGB, with the exception of intellectual circles around Viktor Agartz, had been very much in favour of the ECSC. In practice the trade union leaders had become, if anything, more enthusiastic about European integration as time went on, mainly because it coincided with the economic upswing in Europe, but partly also because of their outstandingly good relations with Monnet. While there is little evidence that the DGB initiated specific SPD views on Europe, it was, like the SPD, more enthusiastic about Euratom. However, its positive attitude became of great importance once the question of European integration had become separated from that of defence.[2] The DGB reinforced the SPD leaders' belief in the necessity for some sort of Euratom, but most importantly, it was fairly influential in persuading Ollenhauer to accept membership of the Action Committee.

The Saar

The attainment of an acceptable solution on the Saar was a precondition of unequivocal SPD commitment to West European integration. The Saar issue was one of the few in which it had been able to count on support inside the government coalition. In 1955 an equable solution in SPD terms looked possible for the first time. To understand the course of developments we have to go back to 1952.

By mid-1952 it had become obvious that many Saarlanders were dissatisfied with their status. The Franco-Saar Conventions, which had been intended to settle the issue, now began to look more like provisional arrangements in need of review. In this situation the French government became enthusiastic about Adenauer's earlier suggestions for a Europeanisation of the Saar. In using a European solution prepared by Adenauer to defend their national interests, the French were only repeating the ECSC sequence. At the same time, the Council of Europe became heavily involved in the issue. Originally concerned with the issue of democratic freedoms in the Saar, on 17 September 1952 the Consultative Assembly accepted a motion by the Dutch Socialist Jonkheer Marinus van der Goes van Naters to include on the agenda consideration of 'the future of the Saar'.[3] This motion was passed to the General Affairs Committee, which appointed van Naters Rapporteur, with only one voice, that of Karl Mommer, the SPD's Saar expert, against this. Karl Mommer suspected van Naters, rightly as it transpired, of Francophilism: 'It is impossible that Herr von Naters will make a good Rapporteur since it is well known that, like Herr Mommer, he has strong views on the Saar Problem.'[4]

While van Naters worked on his plan, the French Government attempted to ensure that any Europeanisation would leave vital French interests intact. On 7 January 1953, Rene Mayer announced that acceptance of a European status for the Saar was a prerequisite for the ratification of the Bonn Agreements and the EDC treaty.[5] On 20 May the revised Franco-Saar conventions, which gave the Saar government the right to make international agreements and to maintain diplomatic and consular representation abroad, were published. At the urging of the SPD, these conventions were condemned on 26 July 1953 in a debate in the Bundestag.[6] Van Naters' report was finally accepted by the General Affairs Committee

116

of the Consultative Assembly on 26 April 1954, by a margin of seventeen votes to Mommer's negative. Pfleiderer of the FDP abstained.[7] It is easy to see why the SPD disapproved of the final report since, despite some economic concessions to the Germans, it linked Europeanisation of the Saar to the creation of the European political community. Both notions were equally abhorrent to the SPD. Thus the *coup de grâce* to the EDC of August 1954 really meant the end of the Naters plan.

On 9 October 1954, Karl Mommer published an important article in the *Stuttgarter Zeitung*, entitled 'Eine Saarlösung mit dem Risiko der Freiheit'. This article, later referred to as the Mommer Plan, in fact presents no detailed blueprint for the future of the Saar. It is mainly a plea to the Federal government not to agree to an ersatz solution in which the Saar would be Europeanised under the aegis of the WEU. More significant is Mommer's view that the best plan for the German government would be not to advance any views of its own but simply to act as a mouthpiece for the Saarlanders. It is quite obvious from this article that Mommer felt Saar opinion was running strongly against the French.

This view was confirmed by the break-up of the SPS, the pro-French socialist party of the Saar, and the founding of the DPS (later SPD Landesverband Saar) under Kurt Conrad, for long the most prominent pro-SPD Saar socialist. At the first meeting of this body on 27 July 1955, the national SPD expressed its pleasure by sending no less than five prominent members of the Parliamentary Party, Mellies, Wehner, Mommer, Bögler and Jakobs.[8] By mid-1955 the SPD really felt that events in the Saar were turning in its favour. On 23 October 1955, this feeling was seen to be justified when 'Europeanisation' was rejected by 67.2 per cent of the electorate. On 1 January 1957 the Saar was reunited with Germany. The SFIO had always pressed less strongly on the Saar issue than the MRP, and was reconciled to its returning to Germany. With the removal of the Saar issue from the agenda, the last obstacle to better relations between the SPD and SFIO, from the point of view of the SPD, was removed.

The influence of the European Assemblies

The SPD members of the Common Assembly and the Council of Europe Consutative Assembly were undoubtedly very influential in changing the party's mind. The two groups worked together in a committee established in 1954, which was known as the 'Arbeitsgemeinschaft für europäische Zusammenarbeit' (working group for European co-operation). Members of the Common Assembly included Herbert Wehner, Willi Birkelbach, Gerard

Kreyssig and Heinrich Deist. Members of the Consultative Assembly included Erich Ollenhauer, Carlo Schmid, Helmut Kalbitzer and Fritz Erler. The changing attitude of the SPD is most apparent in the Common Assembly. At its first session in September 1952, the SPD announced its non-cooperation with the idea of an ad hoc committee since this would imply support of a 'little Europe' solution.[9] Subsequently, however, it was stressed that this was only directed against the EDC, and that the SPD meant to work for the optimisation of the ECSC.[10] By and large the SPD became more favourable to the ECSC the more Schumacher's death became a thing of the past. In the early years, however, it concentrated on efforts to expand the Community and to improve relations with non-members.[11] At a later date it concentrated on increasing the power of the Assembly and democratising the High Authority.[12] This activity was, however, still accompanied by some hostility to the ECSC, a typical example of which is a biting critique of the ECSC by Willi Birkelbach, 'The Coal and Steel Pool – a European cul de sac' in the *Neuer Vorwärts* of 10 July 1953.

This hostility towards the ECSC was not at all apparent by late 1954. By this time the SPD members were pressing for more, not less, power for the High Authority in the fields of investment and social affairs and full employment.[13] This lessening of opposition to the ECSC is an indication of the extent to which opposition to European integration was losing its socialist character. On 1 December 1954, Willi Birkelbach declared in the Common Assembly that the SPD no longer regarded an extension of integration in the economic field as a threat to reunification.[14] In May 1955, the SPD supported a Common Assembly working group on the question of European integration. The SPD also welcomed the communiqué of the Messina Conference.[15]

The SPD's relationship to the Consultative Assembly had been less happy than with the Common Assembly, since it was the arena where the Saar and (despite its constitution) defence had been discussed. The SPD attitude to the Consultative Assembly improved considerably after the failure of the EDC. In the debate on 7–8 July 1955 both Kalbitzer and Erler spoke in favour of the Messina Communiqué.[16]

It is difficult to assess the importance of the experience gained in the Common Assembly and Consultative Assembly. Certainly one cannot assign the importance to Deist that Haas does.[17] A relatively influential figure in the Schumacher period, he was by 1955 not very important in deciding party policy. Carlo Schmid had also become less important. It would, however, be difficult to overestimate the influence of Wehner, Erler, Mommer and Birkelbach, on SPD policy. They were under four

118

main influences. Firstly, they realised that the ECSC had become identified in the public mind with the preservation of German prosperity. Secondly, they came into contact with other politicians, particularly socialists, who were committed to European integration.[18] Thirdly, they often came into contact with Monnet, who spent a great deal of time when he was President of the High Authority with European parliamentarians, particularly from the SPD. Fourthly, their declining opposition on socialist grounds to European integration was only part of a general process of 'de-ideologicisation' in the Party.

Failure of previous policy

As we saw in Chapter 4, the failure of the SPD in the 1953 election immediately led to a demand for a revision of the party's European policy.[19] The resistance of Party members, particularly apparent at the Berlin Conference, made this impossible to achieve vis-à-vis defence. It was a different matter, however, in relation to economics, where the party's step-by-step acceptance of economic integration at a European level followed only slightly behind its abandonment of the demand for nationalisation and socialisation of the domestic economy. The Dortmund Aktionsprogramm of September 1952 and the publication Die Europapolitik der SPD of August 1953 were bitterly opposed to the ECSC. One of the few major changes to the Aktionsprogramm at the party's Berlin Conference was to excise the unfavourable reference to the ECSC and insert a fairly positive passage merely asking for its extension.[20] At this same conference Erler spoke against the EDC, but in favour of a more positive policy to the ECSC and the extension of European integration as a whole.[21]

The basic factor influencing the SPD leadership was the tremendous popularity of the European ideal and, to a lesser extent, the European institutions, particularly with young Germans. While Schumacher was alive the party leadership had been unable to make tactical concessions to this feeling because of his bitter opposition. Under Ollenhauer's different, freer style of leadership it was posssible to make some concessions.

Some light can be thrown on this by considering the case of Willi Birkelbach. Birkelbach had been a prominent opponent of the Schuman initiative and had been elected to the Executive at Berlin because of his well-known opposition to rearmament. As his opposition to rearmament waxed, so did his enthusiasm for economic integration. When I asked him why he supported economic integration from late 1954 onwards, he replied that conditions had changed but was unable to pinpoint any specific changes.[22]

Despite its increased enthusiasm for West European integration, the SPD continued to advance its proposals for a Four Power conference, but party leaders were privately not at all optimistic, since the whole thrust of their argument had been that the Soviet Union would lose interest in the prospect of a united Germany after West Germany had been integrated into the Western Alliance system. The failure of the Paulskirche movement and West Germany's entry into NATO really ended any hopes the SPD had in this direction. It did, however, prepare a set of proposals for the Geneva Conference.[23]

This Conference proved to be a dismal failure as regards any prospect of reunification: on 28 July Krushchev stopped in Berlin on his way back to Moscow, and in an important speech in the Lustgarten underlined the lesson of Geneva that the Soviet government did not intend to facilitate reunification under the prevailing conditions.[24] When Chancellor Adenauer visited Moscow in September 1955 he was accompanied by Carlo Schmid, who was very struck by the intransigence of the Soviet government.[25]

The failure of the SPD's German policy and its opposition to rearmament made the prospect of supporting European integration very attractive. The more so since opinion polls indicated that it was supported by a vast majority of the West German people. In the period immediately after mid-1955, SPD opposition was virtually confined to some aspects of defence. In European policy a state of bipartisanship was achieved. There were slight differences in emphases and Ollenhauer attempted to involve the Third World in the German question, but on basic principles there was wide-ranging agreement.

Movement inside the party

There had always been, as we have already noted, opposition to the leadership policy from politicians within the party who had believed Western European integration as important as German reunification. With the exceptions of Reuter and Kaisen (until 1950) none of this group had been elected to the Executive. They were all members of the MSEUE, the Socialist Movement for the United States of Europe founded by André Philip. Apart from Kaisen, the most important members were Otto Bach (Berlin), Hermann Brill, and Johannes van Nes Ziegler (the chairman of the young socialists). They held their first really large meeting in Frankfurt on 14–15 November 1953. The meeting was attended by 120 delegates, but not a single deputy. A eight-point communiqué based on an address by Kaisen was adopted unanimously:

1   The creation of a new Europe can be brought about more rationally by a return to the old socialist conceptions of European unity at a political and economic level.
2   A decisive task for the new democratic Europe is to convince the Great Powers of the necessity of detente and German unity.
3   A neutralist position is impossible. A European Defence Community would be better for all, including the Soviet Union, than participation by individual European countries in NATO.
4   The real alternative is between a national and a European army.
5   A national army is completely out of date.
6   Democracy had a right to be defended.
7   EDC would provide a democratic framework for EDC.
8   Britain must be persuaded to join and there must be no discrimination against Germany.[26]

Kaisen, Bach, Brill, van Nes Ziegler and K. Peter Schulz were elected to the most important positions on the Committee.

As a counter to this meeting, the Executive announced on 12 December the formation of a European Working Group. Although it included people other than representatives to the European Assemblies, it did not include any of the rebels. This body, known officially as the Arbeitsgemeinschaft für Europäische Fragen (working group for European questions), held its first meeting on 18 January 1954.

On 14 February 1954 a large conference was held in Bremen by the German section of the Socialist Movement for the United States of Europe and the 'Arbeitsthesen zur Europäischen Integration' were published. These requested *inter-alia* an acceleration of European integration, the realisation of European political authority with a supranational directorate and a directly elected parliament, the participation of the SPD in the ad hoc committee of the ECSC.[27]

In 1954, with the election of Birkelbach and the failure of the EDC, the SPD Executive broadened the basis of the Arbeitsgemeinschaften (working groups) and allowed some of the rebels, notably Kaisen, to participate.[28] On 22 November 1954, the Executive published 'Richtlinien für Europa — Arbeitsgemeinschaften'. SPD members specially interested in Europe were to be allowed to form 'working groups', in which members of other parties could participate — a great concession by the Executive, which had refused to consider the fifteen theses of the Berlin students because not all the signatories were SPD members. The results of the deliberations of these bodies were to be sent to the Executive who would make the final decisions.[29]

The SPD Executive remained very suspicious of the German section of the Socialist Movement even after this decision. In the letter already mentioned, Ollenhauer rejected Mollet's suggestion that the Executive might use MSEUE. 'Their relationship to the German party has been very bad because of the clumsy behaviour of the Movement in the past'.[30] For this reason the influence of this opposition on the party's change of course must be reckoned as pretty small.

Much more important was the conversion of Erler, Birkelbach and Wehner to the idea of further integration. Wehner especially had a great deal of influence on Ollenhauer, who remained very lukewarm emotionally about European integration. In the course of time reconciliation eventually took place between the 'Europeans' and the Party Executive, and by 27 January 1956 Herbert Wehner was addressing the newly formed Hamburg Arbeitsgemeinschaft für europäische Fragen on its 'European' tasks.[31]

The Messina Conference

After the failure of the EDC, the Benelux countries drafted a memorandum in the spring of 1955 calling for a Relance Européenne in the economic field. A conference of foreign ministers was held on 1–2 June 1955, when it was agreed in principle to establish a customs' union and a European atomic energy agency. An 'interministerial committee' under Paul Henri Spaak was instructed to give these proposals concrete form.

These two proposals were very much in line with SPD thinking as it had developed in the Common Assembly. The first official reaction was given by Herbert Wehner in the Common Assembly on 24 June 1955. It is significant that he spoke in the name of the whole socialist group.[33] Wehner began by referring to the 'prise de position' of the socialist group on 14 May, when it had been agreed that it was not only possible to integrate coal and steel; the goal ought rather to be an overall synchronised policy. The SPD had always been critical of partial integration. 'Our policy has been to insist on the necessity for a common commercial policy, the creation of a Common Market and the co-ordination of monetary policies.'[33] So much had the SPD attitude altered by this time that Wehner regretted that no mention of the ECSC had been made in the communiqué.

Wehner particularly welcomed the proposals for Euratom, which he thought ought to have priority. This organisation should be directed by a supranational authority and controlled by a democratic parliament. While Wehner considered that Euratom ought to have priority, he recognised that the proposals for the creation of a Common Market were of more far-reaching importance. What the socialist group wanted was the harmonisation of financial and social policy and the co-ordination of monetary policy. It specifically wished to suggest an adaptation fund, a European investment bank and the extension of the powers of the Assembly.[34]

At the fifth sitting of the Consultative Assembly of the Council of Europe on 7 July 1955, Karl Mommer, the SPD's Saar expert, welcomed the Messina Resolutions though he regretted that the Conference had not taken place under the aegis of the Council of Europe.[35] Helmut Kalbitzer, in the Consultative Assembly on 8 July, also welcomed the Messina Resolutions.[36] He claimed that supranationalist and inter-governmental methods were no longer opposed; the question was to find the right method to tackle each individual question as it arose. He also welcomed the idea of a European investment fund. Kalbitzer, a Hamburg representative, was still worried about the Six's links with the rest of Europe and wanted to co-ordinate the plans of the Six more clearly with OEEC. One specific suggestion of Kalbitzer was to make members of the Common Assembly members of the Consultative Assembly.

On 8 July 1955, Wehner welcomed the Messina Resolutions in the Bundestag in similar terms to those used in his speech in the Common Assembly.[37]

The Messina Resolutions, comprehensive in nature and with a smaller explicitly supranational content than the ECSC and EDC, could be expected to appeal to the SPD. I would not, however, assign tremendous importance to this. The SPD's attitude for and against supranationalism had oscillated wildly. Euratom was an example of sectoral integration which the SPD had traditionally disapproved of and which, as Wehner later indicated, really did discriminate against Germany; yet the SPD supported it more than it did the EEC.[38]

The Monnet Committee

This is probably the most difficult influence of all to assess, Monnet's method of wherever possible operating by telephone having heightened the normal difficulties of measuring pressure. His influence acted on the SPD in at least three ways. Firstly, there was the extraordinarily good relationship which had developed between Monnet and the German trade unionists. In the words of Max Kohnstamm, at that time secretary of the High Authority, 'Their trade union friends told them that they got more information in Luxembourg about what was going on in German heavy industry than they ever had obtained at home.' Monnet never tired of explaining the need for and the way towards European unity. On closer acquaintance there seemed to be nothing sinister about either the man or his concept, and very few of the leading politicians and trade unionists failed during those years in Luxembourg to discuss with him, both privately and at length, the European problems of the day. They never found him seeking power, or keeping secret from one the thoughts which he had exposed to another. They also found him open to their own questions and problems, not brushing these aside but trying to relate them to the common task and problem of uniting Europe. The grapevine, the secret telegraph which later seemed to link 'good Europeans' in every one of the six countries, and which contributed so much to the success of European integration, owed its origin to these conversations.[39]

Secondly, there was the trust between Monnet and the SPD delegates to the Assemblies. Much of the credit here belongs to Max Kohnstamm. Kohnstamm, a Dutch socialist, ex-minister concerned with occupation questions, and Dutch negotiator in the Schuman talks, carried out all negotiations with the German parties for Monnet. Less committed to America than Monnet, less interested in military questions, he had developed over a long period very close relations with leading SPD figures, particularly Wehner and Erler.[40] As I have already noted, Wehner's role was crucial.

In his invitation to the SPD to participate in the work of the Committee, Monnet had emphasised the creation of Euratom.[41] This idea was very popular both in the trade unions and the SPD.[42] After 1955 the SPD leadership had become almost obsessed with modernisation of the party. It had proved difficult to drop too much of the old programme because of the resistance of party members (as at the Berlin Conference). Atomic power was something modern which everybody agreed on. The trade unions were more interested in Euratom than a Common Market. As well as being attractive to those who wished to modernise the party, it also appealed to those who still possessed socialist pretensions, who wanted it to be under public control and to be used for non-military purposes.

Once the SPD was in the Monnet Committee it did not experience the same difficulties as in the ratification of former treaties. The Monnet Committee provided a forum for co-ordinating its policies with the trade unions. More importantly it provided the SPD with the information on the course of negotiations that the government had failed to divulge in the past.

124

With the entry of the SPD into the Monnet Action in October 1955, any prospect of real opposition to European institutions was over. Some speakers, notably Carlo Schmid, continued to maintain that efforts towards reunification must precede efforts for Western European integration.[43] There was no doubt, however, that priorities had been reversed. German reunification was relegated from the major to a relatively minor theme in the SPD's European policy.

The 'pro-Europeans' in the party, who were identified with the German section of the Socialist Movement for the United States of Europe, went over to the offensive and established a new journal, *Europa-Brücke*, in December 1955. The editorial board was made up of Wilhelm Kaisen, Hermann Brill, Johann van Nes Ziegler and Otto Bach. The journal's purpose was best expressed by Klaus Peter Schulz, who said it was 'to publicise and strengthen the view of Europe as the most important, indeed perhaps the only, common task of socialism'.[44]

In the first SPD statements after the Messina Communiqué, prominence continued to be given to the old demand to extend the community beyond the Six.[45] This demand foundered as always on the rock of British and Scandinavian disinclination to participate. The 1956 Party Conference in Munich did adopt a resolution calling for the extension of the Community — indeed this was the only substantive resolution on Europe, but it was difficult to exert much pressure on the Federal Government in the face of resolute British disinterest.[46]

The conclusion of the Saar plebiscite on 23 October 1955 removed another possible source of disagreement. In late 1955 some concern was expressed regarding the question of colonies (Ollenhauer was, as I have already indicated, attemping to win the support of Third World leaders like Nehru for the German question) but most interest was focussed on Euratom.[47]

The SPD Party Conference in Munich had been treated to a speech by Professor Carlo Schmid on the role of the intellectual in the atomic era and some delegates had spoken in favour of Euratom. The SPD's interest in Euratom was widely shared in a Europe preoccupied with the vulnerability of oil supplies. (Almost as much ink was spilt on the 'energy gap' in the mid-fifties as was to be spilt on the technological gap in the mid-sixties.) The first three Monnet Committee meetings were concerned with Euratom rather than the Common Market. A valuable insight into SPD thinking at the time is given in an unpublished memorandum, 'The Action Committee of Jean Monnet and the development of Euratom', by Herbert Wehner, written for Ollenhauer on 21 July, after the Committee meeting in Paris on 19—20 July 1956.[48]

The Committee had been unable to agree on a resolution and Jean Monnet had been left to develop a new resolution for its September meeting.

> It became apparent that nobody in the committee thought the simultaneous establishment of the Common Market was a precondition for agreement to Euratom though naturally many thought that the exclusively peaceful use of atomic energy has been extinguished by the French standpoint.

This raised not only the whole question of control, but of what the Monnet Committee could still do. At the end of the memorandum Wehner listed four considerations to be kept in mind by the SPD even before the preparation of the Monnet text.

> 1 Guy Mollet had sacrificed the central core of the Committee's resolution on Euratom. In so doing he had endangered the whole *raison d'être* of the Committee.
> 2 The SPD would have to contend with the argument that Germany was being discriminated against. How would the SPD answer when West Germany was in reality being discriminated against?
> 3 The SPD would have to explain why it had endorsed the January resolution and how this resolution had been thwarted. It would have to continue to fight for the original resolution.
> 4 The SPD was really convinced of the necessity of a European atomic organisation as envisaged in the January resolution.

However, Wehner stressed in conclusion that these views were provisional, and in the event the SPD acceded to the Monnet text published on 20 September 1956. This resolution was merely an exposition of the necessity for co-operation, nothing at all being said about the matters in dispute. That the SPD agreed to it is proof positive that the party had lost all taste for 'opposition' on European matters.

On 22 October Euratom was again discussed in the Consultative Assembly. Helmut Kalbitzer began with a disarmingly frank admission of the SPD's *volte-face*, saying 'We are now passing from the earlier ideology concerning Europe to a more pragmatically oriented policy.'[49] While the Federal government was in favour of fissile material being allowed to fall into private hands, the SPD would insist, on political and economic grounds, that the fissile material be publicly owned. In order to make progress on Euratom, the link between it and the Common Market ought not to be made a precondition of such progress.

On the Common Market itself, there were five main areas of discussion:

the economic organisation of the proposed Common Market, the effect on reunification, the membership of the Common Market. its links with other countries, and parliamentary control. I propose to discuss these *en bloc* instead of dealing with each debate individually, since the SPD did not alter its basic attitude throughout.

On economic organisation the SPD was fairly typical of the socialist parties of the Six as a whole. The SPD asked fairly consistently for a common monetary, financial and investment policy.[50] Where it diverged from the SFIO was on the question of social harmonisation. Some SPD members like Birkelbach complained that Germany's competitive position would weaken if it accepted full scale harmonisation, whereas others saw it as a way of achieving some of the goals of the DGB.[51] Many SPD deputies, particularly from trading centres, were worried by the Common External Tariff.[52] In short, SPD views were indistinguishable from those of the progressive wing of the CDU.

The commitment to reunification weakened to a mere aspiration. Statements were restricted to pious declarations that the question of reunification must not be forgotten or delayed by European integration.[53] Two deputies, Birkelbach and Deist, raised the question as to whether West Germany's integration into an economic community which did not include East Germany would not lead to a deepening of the German division, only to reject the proposition. This had only been true, they concluded, when integration was seen in predominantly military terms.[54] The SPD in common with the FDP, was concerned lest there be any barriers to inter-zonal trade.[55] Some obeisance to earlier SPD standpoints was made in the SPD request that German freedom to leave the Community in case of reunification be specifically written into the treaties.[56]

One of the strongest planks in the Schumacher critique had been the restricted nature of a Europe of the Six. After Messina, the SPD continued to speak in terms of the extension of the Six, but was quashed by British disinterest. On the question of a free trade area, the Erhard wing of the CDU was, if anything, nearer to the United Kingdom government's position. Birkelbach was typical of SPD speakers in claiming that ratification of the EEC had to come before a free trade area.[57] Towards the close of negotiations, some SPD members took fright at the high level of the Common External Tariff and embraced the idea of a free trade area.[58] All that remained of the Schumacher legacy was a bitter distrust of the French on the part of some members.

It is, however, in relation to the last two areas that the SPD policy is most distinctive in emphasis, if not content. In relation to non-member countries, the SPD, as early as October 1955, pointed to the problems raised by the overseas territories and colonies of members, and was worried about the possible economic obligations non-colonial countries would incur through the possession of colonies by others.[59] By the time the arrangements for association were concluded in 1957, Franco-German relations had been improved so much by the return of the Saar that even Karl Mommer said that the final treaty provisions regarding association had alleviated his earlier fears.[60] The SPD's official view that the association agreements be carried out in accordance with the United Nations Charter, that nothing should be done to hinder the overseas territories from attaining independence as soon as possible, that representatives of the territories should be consulted about the Common Market treaty and development aid given generously, not only to the associated areas, but to all under-developed countries, was noticeably more liberal in emphasis than the government's.[61] This liberal emphasis was, however, contradicted by a few party members, who thought that the funds to be invested in the overseas territories could be used more advantageously in Germany or in Europe.[62]

The SPD's view of the need for more democracy in European institutions had not changed, and it continued to lay considerably more emphasis on the need for parliamentary control.[63]

By 1957 the final form of the treaties was almost fixed. A fairly accurate picture of attitudes in the SPD leadership, which can best be characterised as one of critical support, can be gained from Herbert Wehner's article 'Europa mit Einschränkungen und Vorbedingungen − Fragen zum Gemeinsamen Markt'.[64] Wehner was critical of the lack of power to be enjoyed by the proposed European parliament.

Wehner also remained critical of the French government's attitude towards Euratom: public control continued to be a necessity. In his view, workers were insufficiently represented in the Community as the Social and Economic Council was too weak.

The first reading of the treaties passed though the Bundesrat on 3 May 1957, and the Bundestag on 9 May. On 7 May, the Monnet Committee called for speedy ratification. The SPD Parliamentary Party decided on 24 June 1957 to support ratification.

In the debate on 5 July, the SPD supported the government. Indeed the three parties supporting ratification, the CDU, the SPD and the German Party, at first planned to move a common resolution, but the CDU and the SPD could not agree on the wording, and the SPD then moved its own resolution. The two resolutions, however, were almost identical in substance and even in wording. The SPD resolution, for example, spoke of furthering the 'independence' of the overseas territories; the CDU resolution, of their 'political autonomy' (Entscheidungsfreiheit). Another difference was that the CDU resolution mentioned interzonal trade and the position of Berlin; the SPD resolution did not.[65]

The support of both Christian Democrats and Socialists made final ratification a foregone conclusion. At the end of the debate a large majority ratified the treaties by a show of hands. Both the FDP and the Gesamtdeutscher Block/Bund der Heimatvertriebenen und Entrechteten opposed ratification and took exception to French demands and to compromises with them. Robert Margulies, the FDP's foreign trade expert, charged that the Common Market would create a tariff wall around the Six, divide the European market, spread the atmosphere of delay and protectionism that was weakening France, and finally, leave Germany dependent upon French acquiescence to reunification.

On 19 July, the Bundesrat unanimously ratified both treaties.

Conclusions on SPD policy, 1949−57

Any conclusions drawn about the nature of a party's policy in opposition must necessarily be tentative. It is, for instance, much harder than in the case of a governing party, where reference can be made to governmental actions to establish exactly what the policy is. One can turn also to official documents to find out a governing party's policy; with an opposition party it is much harder to fix which pronouncements are authoritative. To establish SPD policy in this period, it was necessary therefore to look at the records of all the important party institutions. It is possible, when talking about the SPD in this period, to be more authoritative than one can usually be in studies of political parties, given the wealth of information available, but even here there are significant gaps, particularly with the non-accessibility of the Protocols of the Party Executive.

One can, however, be fairly certain, in the light of evidence presented in the body of this work about our first hypothesis, namely that domestic considerations played a major role in determining the party's European policy. The most basic of these domestic considerations, Schumacher's general stance on 'opposition', was as we have seen related to a series of assumptions about the political volatility of the German masses. However, one must add here that this was combined in the field of foreign affairs with another set of assumptions about the likely responses of the occupying powers. Schumacher would, in fact, have found the distinction hard to make, since he thought of foreign policy primarily in terms of its impact on the German domestic scene − a view with some validity given West Germany's contingent, dependent sovereignty.

The contest over foreign policy is at the same time the contest over internal policy and the social content of the political order ... Foreign policy sets the limits to the possibilities of our economic and social policy.[66]

Entry into European organisations was therefore rejected, because of what he conceived to be the likely harmful effects on German domestic politics. British entry, for instance, was necessary not for 'power' reasons, but to strengthen social democracy in Germany, to prevent German internal policy being determined purely by reactionary forces. His period of leadership is marked by a fanatical desire to establish democracy on the right lines in Germany. Such a policy demanded in his view a ruthless concentration on Germany and seeing things from a purely German and socialist standpoint.

Under Ollenhauer short-term, purely tactical considerations played a much larger role. Where Schumacher had relied on moral force, Ollenhauer put his money on tactics. It was a period, as a veteran SPD functionary remarked to me, of 'Anpassung' (adjustment). However, at no point in this eight-year period am I convinced that the form a particular European institution took was of primary importance in determining the SPD's attitude. Its attitudes towards supranationalism oscillated wildly.[67] The Council of Europe was condemned for not being supranationalist enough. The Coal and Steel Community was, in contrast, held to be too supranationalist, though even here the party was confused and we find Nölting, a strong supporter of the party leadership, advocating more supranationalism. Supranationalism was condemned in the EDC and then advocated for the EEC and Euratom. The SPD's support for EEC and Euratom cannot be explained on institutional grounds since they represented just the sort of sectoral integration exercise, confined to a Europe of the Six, about which the SPD had often complained so bitterly.

What remained constant was the SPD's habit of seeing things in purely German terms. It is difficult to decide, as the name implies, whether to assign 'Deutschlandpolitik' to the realm of foreign or domestic policy. It must be considered as foreign policy in that it is ultimately dependent on other members of the international system for its realisation. On the other hand, it was not seen by the SPD to belong truly to the sphere of foreign affairs, and progress in this area was desired by Schumacher for primarily domestic political reasons.

One can be reasonably confident that, rather than the inherent attractions of the institutions themselves, it was the demonstrable failure of any progress towards German unity, indeed a worsening of its prospects following West German entry into NATO, that made possible the change in party direction. This argument should not however be pushed too far. The institutions did of themselves possess some attractive qualities, particularly their identification with economic prosperity. It is on this point that the views expressed by Haas have some validity.[68] The successful functioning of the ECSC did help to reinforce the popularity of the European ideal in West Germany and thus bring about the SPD *volte-face.*

As the prospects for German unity faded, 'Deutschlandpolitik' tended to become identified more with foreign than domestic policy. It is also an indication of the process of change, of 'de-ideologicisation' in the SPD, that the nature of opposition on domestic grounds changed in emphasis. Under Schumacher's leadership opposition was pursued on the grounds of the effect it would have on socialism in West Germany and German unity. Under Ollenhauer the arguments about the effect on the prospects of socialism within West Germany, became considerably muted, except in relation to rearmament.

It is more difficult to express firm conclusions as to the nature of this SPD opposition, though there is no doubt as to its concentration, under Schumacher, on foreign policy.[68]

Despite superficial appearances to the contrary, Schumacher's intransigent opposition had something of a rhetorical symbolic quality. There was never any danger the SPD would not accept majority decisions of the Bundestag or carry on extra-parliamentary opposition, and when he skirted the bounds of unconstitutionality with his 'Bundeskanzler der Alliierten' (Chancellor of the Allies) speech on 24 November 1949, he apologised very quickly and little more was heard of a 'policy of intransigence'. Although Schumacher laid great stress on reunification, the virulence of his anti-communism meant that his loyalty, and the loyalty of the SPD, to the West German state was never really in doubt. In the last analysis he would always prefer a separate democratic West Germany to a re-unified communist Germany. Given the lack of fundamental difference between Schumacher and Adenauer, his opposition resembled, in content if not always in style, the classic English model more than the opposition of principle model. His rejection of the opposition of principle strategy meant that once he had been outvoted he had no alternative but to accept the majority verdict and the consequent loss of face.

There is no doubt then that Schumacher saw himself as a loyal opposition leader. There was some necessary ambiguity involved here since, in the theory of the time, neither opposition leader, nor indeed the Chancellor, were expected to render ultimate loyalty to the Federal Republic — this being reserved for a future re-united Germany. Moreover, any opposi-

131

tion leader would have been likely to stress the dangers of sacrificing the national option in escaping some of the consequences of dependent sovereignty.[70] Yet, as we have seen, the virulence of his anti-communism meant that his loyalty and the loyalty of the SPD to the West and the West German state was pretty well absolute. This identification with the West, combined with a desire to preserve the national option, blurred the edges of his 'Alternativepolitik' and resulted in the SPD's being distrusted by those both to the right and left of it, and its inability to fulfil Schumacher's claim that it would always present concrete alternatives to government policy.

> The tactically meant and tactically understood combination of economic and foreign policy, between 1949 and 1953, might in detail have been reasonably and skilfully based, but it was branded by a lack of purpose. Only this lack of purpose made the 'No' of the SPD so objectionable. It was not so much the party's 'No' which damaged it but rather the fact that the 'No' was a half 'Yes' — the dilemma of the SPD's 'Yes, but' is inescapable. (R. Petry)

With Schumacher's death, a policy of opposition focussed on parliament became increasingly difficult to maintain. It had depended on the SPD's possessing a leader who could challenge and indeed defeat Adenauer in parliamentary duels. It very quickly became apparent that Ollenhauer was unable to fulfil this requirement. One result was to broaden the nature of opposition — to engage in a legal duel with the government.

The relaxation of tension, and the attempt by the Soviet Union to seduce the Germans away from the EDC by offering them a chance of reunification, presented the SPD with real difficulties. Schumacher's virulent anti-communism had rendered his commitment to German unity purely rhetorical. With the change in the Soviet attitude the SPD was now placed in a position where a failure to respond to Soviet advances would have exposed the hollowness of its claims to be the only party to put German unity first. Ollenhauer's response in advocating the testing of Soviet intentions, while stressing the necessity for free elections, was probably the best that could be done. Even this slight concession rebounded on the SPD after the uprising of 17 June. It also angered revisionist members of the party just at a time when left-wing members were annoyed about the abandonment of some economic shibboleths.

The alternative of bipartisanship in foreign policy, while in some ways attractive, proved even more elusive. Adenauer, despite the crocodile tears in his *Memoirs*, needed an SPD opposition in foreign policy to weld the CDU/CSU — a heterogeneous collection of classes in search of an ideology

— into a coherent unity.[71] More fundamentally, the salience of the defence question, unpopular both with the electorate and the SPD rank and file, prevented such a step being taken. In the opposition to rearmament there were times when the SPD opposition appeared as one of principle. This was particularly true of the Paulskirche movement. However, that did not have the full support of the SPD behind it, and leading SPD members lacked credibility as demonstrators. It cannot really be regarded as an 'opposition of principle', since this implies a complete rejection of the system. Nevertheless, it is important, since its failure prevented the SPD from adopting such a strategy, by discrediting the militants who had been strengthened by the Berlin Conference, and allowed the SPD to participate in the drafting of legislation for the new German forces. The failure of the Paulskirche movement was thus crucial to the later development of the SPD, since it made possible the acceptance of the view, later to be identified with Wehner, that SPD influence was heightened by collaboration with, rather than opposition to, the government.

The participation in the Monnet Committee removed some of the disadvantages of opposition. It gave the SPD access to information (without which it was very difficult to frame alternatives) and the appearance of responsibility. Opposition was henceforward restricted to a 'Bereichsopposition', one confined to some areas. As a matter of strategy it suffered from the disability of being unclear to the average voter, and it did not bring the SPD any real success in the 1957 elections.

The increased influence of Wehner and Erler reflected important changes in the distribution of power in the SPD. As long ago as 1958 Klaus Peter Schulz, in *Opposition als politisches Schicksal*, drew attention to the loss of power by the party functionaries in this period. While Schumacher was alive, he had been Chairman of both the Party Executive and the Parliamentary Party. In fact he relied heavily on the apparatchiki, Ollenhauer, Nau, Heine, Eichler, Mellies and Schoettle. After his death the apparatchiki sharing the ideological conservatism of the rank and file continued to exert a lot of influence, much as they had done in the period before World War I. However, the failure of the Paulskirche movement and Ollenhauer's poor performance in parliament led to the Parliamentary Party's displaying greater independence of the Executive. This movement reached a climax in 1957 at a Parliamentary Party meeting on 30 October. At this meeting a majority of the deputies accepted a resolution opposed by Ollenhauer. Rejecting the official proposal to re-elect the existing leadership or to add a third vice-chairman, the deputies agreed to elect three new vice-chairmen. The rebels proposed three candidates, Schmid, Wehner and Erler. They were elected. Schoettle, incumbent Vice-Chairman and

133

Ollenhauer's choice for re-election, sensed the outcome and refused to run. Mellies was defeated.

The growing influence of the Parliamentary Party had important repercussions on European policy. It was not so much, as Mahant claims, 'a matter of generations' as a matter of attitudes and roles. Wehner, Erler, Schmid, and indeed the Parliamentary Party in general, were professional politicians dependent on elections. This gave them quite a different attitude to change from the paid functionaries who still saw the SPD as a 'movement' party. I have not had access to the Protocols of the Party Executive, but interviews with Schoettle, Eichler and Schmid have left me in no doubt as to the greater support for European integration in the Parliamentary Party, rather than the Executive. Ollenhauer is very important in this connection, as he was able to get the Executive to accept the ideas of the Parliamentary Party, the members of the Executive considering him by temperament and experience closer to them.

Any opinion on the merit of the SPD's ideas on Europe in the early years of the Federal Republic must involve a large speculative element. Schumacher's calculation that premature acceptance of an unjust position for Germany might bring temporary benefits that would eventually turn sour looked pretty unconvincing in Adenauer's golden years after 1957. On the other hand, the erection of the Berlin Wall, the weak Western response to this step, and the rise of an extreme nationalist movement, the NPD, after 1966, appeared to lend *post hoc* credence to Schumacher's views. On balance though, Adenauer's decision to begin transforming Germany's dependent sovereignty, even if it meant accepting a junior position, was probably correct. It is much less clear that his attitude of continual concessions to the French over the Saar should not have built up as a focus of resentment.

Schumacher's fundamental miscalculation was his inability to believe that a free-market economy could achieve the success it did. It was this prosperity, not Schumacher's nationalist rhetoric, that neutralised the refugees, compensated for any discrimination against Germany in the European institutions, rendered irrelevant the SPD demand for greater workers' participation in them, and indeed consolidated the West German state. It was in fact only a temporary check in this prosperity that gave the NPD a chance.

It is more difficult to decide on the merits of the SPD's preoccupation with reunification. It did draw large numbers of refugees, on whose support the SPD could probably not otherwise have counted. It did provide the party with a possible source of leverage on the governing coalition, particularly with the FDP. It successfully insulated the SPD against the

134

sort of attacks made on it after World War I. It is hard to imagine that the present day 'Ostpolitik' would have been possible had not the SPD passed through such a period.

Yet the disadvantages of such a policy are equally obvious. The subordination of all foreign policy questions to their effects on 'Deutschlandpolitik' resulted in an almost invariably negative attitude. This made it difficult for the SPD to identify itself with Adenauer's foreign policy successes. As the prospects of unification dimmed, the party's concentration on unity made it more and more difficult for it to *present concrete alternatives tuned to concrete situations*. At the same time the pursuit of unification began to partake of a certain lack of immediacy and practicability. This was in sharp contrast to the tangible economic and political benefits flowing from the government's 'Westpolitik'. In these circumstances the Adenauer solution (also the solution of 'Europeans' like Kaisen in the SPD) of pressing ahead with Western European integration while preserving German unity as an 'aspiration', in the sense used by Arnold Wolfers, was very effective. Western European integration, which was attractive to West German voters both at the level of idealism and 'gut-politics' was thus catered for, while the strong national and theoretical attachment to a unified Germany was left largely intact.

The SPD opposition to rearmament was, as I have shown in Chapter 4, riddled with ambiguities and contradictions, particularly after Schumacher's death. The more intransigent its policy became, the less effect it had on developments. This led at least to a partial change in policy in 1956, when it participated in the framing of the legislation for the Bundeswehr. Given the strength of opposition to rearmament, particularly in South Germany, it was probably necessary for the party to adopt the course it did on rearmament. Recent scholarly opinion has tended to confirm the SPD's claim that Russian intentions on German unity after 1952 were fairly serious. What is less clear is whether it would have been wise for the Federal government to test these intentions, given the hostile attitude of the United States government. Given the impracticability of their implementation, the SPD's schemes on collective security in the period 1954–55 cannot be accorded much importance. It is noteworthy that even present-day leaders like Wehner and Brandt do not go back to them when seeking to give some definition to their concepts of a 'European peaceful order'. The SPD's insistence on British entry withered on the vine in face of resolute British disinterest.

The SPD's views on European integration did have a valuable impact on the EEC in two ways; Euratom unfortunately has never really functioned as envisaged by its founders. The SPD's interest in the Third World had an impact on the negotiations and was one of the catalysts of the Community's association policy. More importantly, the SPD had consistently insisted on the necessity for as much democracy as possible in Community institutions. This is one facet of its policy which has never altered. Whatever else can be said for or against the SPD, this deep attachment to democratic norms has been its most enduring contribution to European and German political life.

Notes

[1] See Ritter op. cit., Edinger op. cit., and Heino Kaack 'Das Problem einer aussenpolitischen Alternative für Deutschland. Ein Beitrag zur Analyse der Anfänge der deutschen Aussenpolitik nach 1945 unter besonderer Berücksichtigung der Konzeption Kurt Schumachers' Phil. Diss., Kiel 1965. The theses of Scherzinger and Shears both deal with the earlier period. However, for some interesting observations see Edelgard Mahant 'French and German Attitudes to the Common Market Negotiations' Ph.D., London 1969.

[2] Mahant, op. cit., pp. 354–71.

[3] R.H. Schmidt, *Die Saarpolitik 1949–57* vol. 2, Berlin 1961, p. 569. Schmidt's book deals exhaustively with all aspects of the Saar problem.

[4] Ibid., p. 569.

[5] *FAZ*, 8 January 1953.

[6] See Chapter 4 above.

[7] Schmidt, op. cit., vol. 2, p. 575.

[8] Schmidt, op. cit., vol. 3, p. 271.

[9] Proceedings of the ECSC Common Assembly, Opening Session, 1st Sitting, 12 September 1952, p. 84 (H. Wehner).

[10] Proceedings of the ECSC Common Assembly, 4th Sitting, 17 September, p. 372-4 (C. Schmid).

[11] Proceeding of the Common Assembly, 14 June 1953, p. 11f (H. Wehner); 20 June 1954, p. 1ff (G. Kreyssig); 14 May 1954, pp. 143, 150-3ff (H. Wehner).

[12] Proceeding of the ESCS Common Assembly, 4th Sitting, 16 June 1953, p. 2ff (H. Wehner); 6th Sitting, 20 June 1953, p. 1ff (G. Kreyssig); 4th Sitting, 14 May 1954, p. 160ff (H. Wehner).

[13] E.B. Haas, op. cit., p. 137; SPD *Jahrbuch*, 1954–55, p. 17ff.

[14] Proceedings of the ECSC Common Assembly, 1 December 1954, pp. 97–9 (W. Birkelbach).

[15] Proceedings of the ECSC Common Assembly, 24 June 1955,

p. 609−11 (H. Wehner).

16 Proceedings of the Council of Europe Consutative Assembly, 7th Session, 6th Sitting, 7 July 1955, pp. 112−116 (K. Mommer); 8th Sitting, 8 July 1955, pp. 231−5 (H. Kalbitzer).

17 Haas, op. cit., p. 130.

18 See letter, Erler − Ollenhauer, 2 November 1955, discussing the results of meeting with Mollet and Birkelbach (Nachlass Ollenhauer, correspondence, J.39).

19 See Chapter 4.

20 Flechtheim, op. cit., vol. 3, pp. 96−7.

21 See *Protokoll des Berliner Parteitages*, pp. 79−80 (F. Erler).

22 Interview with W. Birkelbach, Wiesbaden, November 1966.

23 'Programm der Sozialdemokratischen Partei Deutschlands zu den Viermächteverhandlungen über die deutsche Wiedervereinigung' published by the SPD Executive on 9 May 1955.

24 D. Dallin, *Soviet Foreign Policy after Stalin*, London 1960, p. 283.

25 Interview with Carlo Schmid, Bonn, July 1967.

26 *FAZ*, 16 November 1953. See also *Informationsdienst* no. 96 of Europa Union.

27 *FAZ*, 15 February 1954.

28 Interview with Kaisen, November 1966.

29 This document was filed under J.39 (Nachlass Ollenhauer, European questions after 1945).

30 Letter, Erler − Ollenhauer. See note 18 above.

31 See *FAZ*, 28 January 1956.

32 Proceedings of the ECSC Common Assembly, 24 June 1955, pp. 609−11 (H. Wehner).

33 Ibid., p. 609.

34 Ibid., p. 611.

35 Proceedings of the Council of Europe Consultative Assembly, 5th Sitting, 7 July 1955, pp. 112−16 (K. Mommer).

36 Op. Cit., note 16.

37 Deutscher Bundestag, *Verhandlungen* 8 July 1955, pp. 5415−18 (H. Wehner).

38 See note 48 below.

39 M. Kohnstamm 'The European tide' in S.R. Graubard (ed.) *A New Europe?*, Boston 1964, p. 155.

40 Interview with M. Kohnstamm, Easter 1970.

41 R11A/PEP, Action Committee for the United States of Europe *Statements and Declarations, 1969*, p. 11.

42 See Mahant, section on trade unions, *passim*.

[43]   Carlo Schmid in SPD Parliamentary Party 'Mitteilungen für die Presse' 17 November 1955.

[44]   *Europa-Brücke* no. 1, December 1955, p. 9.

[45]   SPD Pressedienst, 4 June 1955; Deutscher Bundestag, *Verhandlungen*, 8 July 1955, p. 5415 (H. Wehner).

[46]   See *Protokoll der Verhandlungen des Parteitages der SPD*, Munich, p. 350.

[47]   Paul Haupt *Volkswirtschaft*, 31 October 1955. See also SPD Pressedienst, 23 April 1956.

[48]   Nachlass Ollenhauer, Monnet Committee section.

[49]   Proceedings of the Council of Europe Consultative Assembly, 21st Sitting, 22 October 1956, p. 677 (H. Kalbitzer).

[50]   Proceedings of the ECSC Common Assembly, 24 June 1955, pp. 609–11 (H. Wehner).

[51]   Proceedings of the ECSC Common Assembly, 29 November 1956, p. 107 (W. Birkelbach); *Vorwärts*, 11 November 1955.

[52]   W. Deist, *Hamburger Echo*, 9 March 1957.

[53]   Deutscher Bundestag, *Verhandlungen*, 31 January 1957, p. 10,674 (E. Ollenhauer).

[54]   Deutscher Bundestag, *Verhandlungen*, 9 May 1957, p. 12,012 (W. Birkelbach); 5 July 1957, p. 13,341 (H. Deist).

[55]   Resolution of the SPD Parliamentary Party, Deutscher Bundestag, *Verhandlungen*, 21 March 1957 p. 17,381.

[56]   Ibid.

[57]   Deutscher Bundestag, *Verhandlungen*, 9 May 1957, p. 12,011 (W. Birkelbach).

[58]   See note 52 above.

[59]   Cited Mahant, op. cit., p. 313.

[60]   K. Mommer, S.W. Funk, 25 February 1957.

[61]   For details see E. Mahant, op. cit., p. 313.

[62]   For details see E. Mahant, op. cit., p. 313.

[63]   See almost all speeches by SPD speakers in the Common Assembly.

[64]   *Vorwärts*, 22 February 1957.

[65]   Deutscher Bundestag, *Verhandlungen*, 5 July 1957 pp. 13,463–4.

[66]   In 'Die Staatsgewalt geht von den Besatzungsmächten aus' Bonn, N.D. p. 3.

[67]   See especially Chapters 2 and 3 above.

[68]   Haas, op. cit., pp. 131–9.

[69]   W. Kralewski and K. Neunreither, *Oppositionelles Verhalten im ersten Deutschen Bundestag 1949–53*, Cologne 1964, p. 92. (Statutes passed against SPD opposition at first vote: budget – purely formal 78.9 per

cent; foreign affairs 55 per cent; finance 15.4 per cent; economics 7.4 per cent.)

70 J. Frankel, *National Interest*, London 1970, pp. 31–3, where he points out that oppositions tend to articulate long term national interests, while governments are more oriented towards capabilities. On the specific West German situation, see W. Paterson, 'State and Nation in post-war Germany', PSA paper, 1972, published as 'Foreign Policy and Stability in West Germany' *International Affairs*, July 1973, pp. 413–30.

71 See A. Heidenheimer, 'Foreign Policy and Party Discipline in the CDU' *Parliamentary Affairs*, 1959, pp. 70–84.

6 The SPD and European Integration 1958-73

Since the establishment of the Common Market and Euratom, SPD policy on European integration has necessarily lacked some of the dramatic qualities it displayed in the early years of the Federal Republic. It is, nevertheless, full of interest. In the following chapter I shall focus on four main themes connected with the SPD's European policy since 1958: the SPD's response to the Gaullist challenge to Community institutions, its changing attitudes to the institutional forms of the Communities, its view of third countries, and the relationship between its West European policy and 'Ostpolitik'.

In the late fifties the main thrust of SPD policies was focussed on the 'Campaign against Atomic Death' (an SPD — led campaign for the barring of atomic weapons on German soil) and East—West relations. Interest in the developing EEC though warm, was spasmodic, and support for the Brussels institutions was tempered by a desire for a less restrictive economic organisation that would allow Britain to participate. There was thus some support in the SPD for the British notion of a wider free trade area, but it was never pushed hard by the party.[1]

The 'Campaign against Atomic Death' had really petered out by late 1958, and the culmination of the SPD initiatives on East—West relations, the Deutschland plan of spring 1959, was very quickly seen to be stillborn. Characteristically, it was Herbert Wehner who most clearly perceived the consequences of these failures and, in a speech in mid summer 1960, he indicated that the SPD was prepared to drop most, if not all, of its old foreign policy demands in favour of bipartisanship. Herbert Wehner's speech can be regarded as really being the foreign policy equivalent to the Bad Godesberg Programme.[2]

The SPD attack on Gaullism

This SPD desire for bipartisanship was very largely fulfilled in the area of East—West relations. It proved much more difficult to achieve, somewhat to the surprise of the SPD, in relation to European integration, where it

141

had considered itself in agreement with the government, i.e. Adenauer, on fundamentals. The problem was that, as Adenauer grew steadily more suspicious of the policy of the United States after the death of Dulles in 1959, he came ever nearer to de Gaulle. This accommodation between de Gaulle and Adenauer scarcely affected Adenauer's view of the correct alliance policy to be followed by the Federal Republic, but it did affect Adenauer's perception of European integration, and as the Gaullist challenge to the European institutions mounted, Adenauer often seemed on the point of undoing some of his earlier achievements in pursuit of Franco-German friendship. In this situation the SPD, paradoxically, found itself criticising de Gaulle in the name of the values it had formerly attacked in Adenauer, those of European integration and unswerving devotion to American policy. The first SPD criticism of Gaullism came in a series of speeches given by SPD leaders in the summer of 1960, attacking the notion of a Gaullist Europe because of its lack of supranationality and democratic control.[3] However, the real flashpoint occured early in 1963. At the time of his rejection, in January 1963, of British entry into the EEC, de Gaulle was engaged in negotiating a treaty providing for very close co-operation between the Federal Republic and France. The climate for this treaty had been skilfully prepared by de Gaulle's trimphal visit to West Germany in the autumn of 1962. In the context of de Gaulle's rejection of British entry at his press conference on 14 January, and his evident hostility towards United States policy, the Franco-German Friendship Treaty was looked on by many as a clear legitimisation by West Germany of French policies.

The treaty was thus seen by the SPD as endangering the twin goals of European integration and the solidarity of the Western Alliance, the goals it had so recently come to share, and the main burden of SPD criticism of the treaty reflected this. However the first criticism of the treaty by a prominent member of the SPD, Kurt Mattick, focussed on its failure to mention German reunification. This was all the more dangerous, in Mattick's view, because of de Gaulle's hostile relations with the United States, since German reunification could only be brought about by the Americans.[4]

The campaign against the treaty was very skilfully orchestrated by Herbert Wehner. Wehner was in a very difficult position. He had played a crucial role in persuading the SPD to change its internal and external policy so that it could become more attractive in electoral terms. This was, however, a long term calculation; in the short run the best hope for the SPD lay in a coalition with the Christian Democrats. The problem now was that Adenauer was endangering both his former policy goals and the

142

unity of the CDU/CSU. In his pro-French policy Adenauer enjoyed the support of the CSU and of South German Catholic ultra-Europeans like von Brentano. The majority in the Parliamentary Party, including Gerhard Schroeder, the Foreign Minister, and Ludwig Erhard, Adenauer's designated successor, were just as clearly against it. Wehner, like the skilful strategist he was, resolved to keep all the options open, and he therefore pressed his opposition to the treaty sufficiently hard to satisfy both the Schroeder/Erhard section of the CDU and the SPD Parliamentary Party, without, however, doing this in such an aggressive manner as to totally alienate Adenauer. Throughout February Wehner insisted that the treaty was only acceptable if it fulfilled three conditions. These were that it was intended to strengthen European unity on the basis of the EEC; that it encouraged a partnership between the United States and the EEC; and that it strengthen NATO rather than become the kernel of a special alliance between France and West Germany.[5] Wehner also suggested that the Federal Republic conclude an analgous treaty with the United Kingdom.[6]

Wehner's freedom of manoeuvre was somewhat circumscribed by the depth of feeling in the SPD against the treaty. This hostility was very obvious in the ratification stage in the Bundesrat, where both the SPD governments of Hamburg and Hesse introduced resolutions that were extremely critical of the treaty. These resolutions asked for new clauses in it that would make it clear that it was in conformity with both the spirit and the letter of the other treaties which had been entered into by the Federal Republic. The resolutions also called for a similar treaty with Britain and for a commitment from the Federal government to pressing the EEC governments for a speedy beginning to trade talks with the United States.[7] The attitude of the SPD as expressed by Wehner accordingly hardened slightly as the date of the first reading approached. A further factor in the SPD's harsher opposition to the treaty was the unanimous opposition to it expressed by the Liaison Bureau of the Socialist Parties of the Six (including the SFIO) at its meeting on 14 March.[8] Wehner gave notice in a series of articles and interviews in early March that the SPD would make its support of the treaty conditional on the acceptance of an additional clause which would make clear that the treaty was to be understood as being in conformity with West Germany's other treaty obligations.[9] In the event, the SPD did not press its demand for an extra clause, but accepted a preamble to the treaty prepared by the FDP.[10] Unlike a new clause this was not binding in international law, but it had the enormous advantage of now requiring new negotiations with the French government. In both parliamentary debates on the treaty the SPD's case was made by Wehner, who successfully managed the difficult task of stating the SPD's objections with great clarity, while yet conveying an ultimately conciliatory attitude to the government.[11]

After the retiral of Adenauer in October 1963, West German foreign policy was made by the Protestant triumvirate of Erhard (Chancellor), Schroeder (Foreign Minister) and von Hassel (Defence Minister). Not surprisingly, they laid a great emphasis on relations with the United States and played down the Franco-German Friendship Treaty. However, although Adenauer had given up the Chancellorship, he continued to act as Party Chairman of the CDU and in the years after 1963 he continually used this position to attack the foreign policy orientation of the government and to plead for a closer identification with France. In this campaign he was supported by Strauss and the CSU and some important CDU members like Gerstenmaier. This struggle between so-called Gaullists and Atlanticists was to dominate public discussion of European policy in the years 1963–65. In this controversy the SPD retained an Atlanticist conviction and statements by SPD leaders in the period 1963–65 are predominantly critical of de Gaulle.[12]

Erler had very close relations with Gerhard Schroeder and was consistently a sharp critic of de Gaulle. Brandt, who was really of lesser importance in the formulation of SPD policy until the election year of 1965, preoccupied as he was with Berlin and without the advantages enjoyed by Erler and Wehner as leaders of the Parliamentary Party, had already begun thinking about the long-term reformulation of West German foreign policy. This caused him to take a kinder view of de Gaulle than the rest of his party. Brandt was as convinced an Atlanticist as Erler and Wehner and he therefore rejected completely the implications of Gaullism for defence. However, in the aftermath of the Berlin Wall, Brandt had become interested in pan-European constructions as well as the integration of Western Europe. In an important speech in New York in May 1964 he therefore praised de Gaulle because of his emphasis on all-European solutions, and though he did not of course, praise de Gaulle's hostility to the European institutions he claimed that the Gaullist check to the supranational integration of Western Europe would make it easier to take up contact with and include the East European states in any future plans.[13] This was a point of view in marked contrast to his more orthodox colleagues, who continued to cling to the view that a strengthened supranational EEC would act as a magnet for the East European states.

By the time of the formation of the Grand Coalition (1966–69) Fritz Erler was dead and foreign policy was clearly made by Willy Brandt, who acted as Foreign Minister. There was, however, an informal division of labour in the government, with the SPD Ministers Brandt and Wehner

144

concentrating on 'Ostpolitik' rather than Western Europe. When Brandt spoke on Western Europe in these years he tended to express himself in safe generalities. Now that West Germany was carrying out an active 'Ostpolitik' of its own, however, Brandt found the necessity for consultation with the French increasingly irksome and he made a biting attack on French defence pretensions in a speech to a Provincial Party Conference of the SPD in Ravensburg on 3 February 1968.[14] This speech caused a minor rupture in Franco-German relations, and relations between the SPD and the Gaullist government remained consistently bad until the SPD formed a new government with the FDP in September 1969.

Attitudes to the European institutions

The dominant SPD concern over the whole period has been to strengthen the democratic element in the European institutions. A minor theme in the early years of the period covered, the SPD demand for the fusion of the three communities, the EEC, Euratom and the ECSC, was fulfilled.[15] The demand for increased rights for the European Parliament was mentioned in the 1961 election campaign and then more strongly in a European Manifesto produced for the 1965 election. This point was, however, common to the SPD, the FDP and large sections of the CDU. That the SPD was more committed to democratising the European institutions than the other West German political parties, became apparent in the great EEC constitutional crisis of summer 1965. The crisis was ostensibly sparked off by a resolution of the European Parliament which provided both for the Commission of the EEC to be financed directly out of customs revenues and for a very significant increase in parliamentary control.[16] The SPD played the major role in the drafting of this resolution and it was moved by Käte Strobel in the name of all the socialists in the European Parliament. A week later the SPD Parliamentary Party moved substantially the same resolution in the Bundestag, again in the name of Frau Strobel. In a resolution on 30 June 1965 on the proposals of the President of the EEC Commission, the Bundestag adopted the main points of the SPD resolution.[17] A resolution prepared by Karl Mommer, providing for the direct election of the West German representatives to the European Parliament, failed in committee.[18] These moves, together with statements from the President of the EEC Commission, so alarmed de Gaulle that he withdrew from the Communities until he was tempted back by the Luxembourg Compromise of 1966.

In power in the Grand Coalition of 1966—69, the SPD devoted relatively little time to the development of plans for the reform of the EEC institutions. There were probably three main reasons for this. Firstly, there was the feeling of relief that France had returned and a desire to let sleeping dogs lie. Secondly it has also always been the case that opposition parties have been more productive than governments in the production of these plans. Thirdly, SPD foreign policy in government was made much more clearly by Brandt, who had other priorities.

Brandt's concentration on 'Ostpolitik' and his desire for all-European institutions had led him to reject the federal model for the development of EEC institutions.[19] In his one major speech on the subject to the EEC Council of Ministers in September 1968, Brandt asked for the further development of economic union, but it is clear from his speech that his conception of economic union was a very loose one, involving much more consultation and co-ordination than at present prevails between the various governments, but stopping far short of what is normally understood by the term.[20]

In his declaration as Chancellor to the Summit Conference in the Hague on 1 December 1969, Brandt again had relatively little to say about the European institutions, apart from a ritual reference to the need for a stronger parliament and more progress towards economic union.[21] Moreover, the general thrust of his speech leaves one in no doubt that he was much more interested in the extension of the Community than in its inner development.

In his second Governmental Declaration on 18 January 1973, Brandt stated that European union was to be the foremost goal of the Federal government. It is not yet clear if this heralds a major change in direction since, although he refers to 'political union', it is merely in terms of greater inter-governmental co-operation. The main emphasis continues to be laid on economic union, again conceived in a fairly loose fashion.[22]

The waning of the party's interest in the Brussels institutions since it became part of the government in 1966 provoked relatively little internal controversy. The only public dispute on the issue in the party occurred in October 1971, over the question of direct elections for the European Parliament. The decision of the SPD Parliamentary Party to drop its former policy by which West Germany would proceed unilaterally to direct elections in favour of one which involved waiting until a common European Community approach had been worked out on 'grounds of fairness to the new members' provoked the resignation of Klaus Peter Schulz.[23]

Unlike the situation in the British Labour Party, the left in the SPD is basically committed to the EEC, since it sees it as the only possible

146

mechanism for controlling multinational companies. Its most prominent member, Jochen Steffen, actually campaigned in Norway in the Referendum campaign in favour of Norwegian entry. Steffen is particularly keen on the control of multinational companies, and to this end he hopes to set up an EEC-wide information pool on their activities.

Attitudes towards third countries

The opposition of the SPD to Gaullism involved a very positive attitude towards the United States and Britain. Indeed, Wolfram Hanrieder has pointed out the similarities between the views of the SPD and the United States government on Europe.[24] This identification with United States policy is of course a characteristic of all SPD foreign policy in the 1960s. There were three main reasons for this development. Firstly, two of the SPD's most important leaders were particularly impressed by the necessity of close identification with the United States – Brandt, because of the special position of Berlin, and Erler, because of his interest in and knowledge of strategic questions (Erler's role in the party was taken over, after his death in 1966, by Helmut Schmidt, who shared the same interests). Secondly, the mere fact of Adenauer's change of heart left a useful area to be exploited, given the very strong emotional identification of the great majority of West Germans with the United States. Thirdly, the SPD did not have the same strong commitment to the West German farming community, and thus the Common Agricultural Policy, as the FPD and CDU. It was, of course, the Common Agricultural Policy that was the main bone of contention in EEC–US relations.

In relation to the choice between an Atlantic or Gaullist orientation for Europe, SPD policy was, uncharacteristically, totally consistent. The party supported John Kennedy's idea of a European–Atlantic Partnership.[25] The party leadership also rejected any European atomic force unless in partnership with the United States – a position which made it an enthusiastic supporter of the ill-fated MLF project of the United States government.[26] In its European Manifesto of July 1964 the party suggested the establishment of another EEC Commission purely to liaise with the United States.[27] This desire for close relations with the United States has remained a constant in SPD policy up until the present.

Similarly, the SPD's commitment to British entry was significantly stronger than that of the CDU and FDP. When the EEC decided to proceed to the 'second stage' of the Common Market in January 1962, the SPD supported this step, but at the same time urged EEC members to avoid the danger of an 'inexpedient autarchy' that would jeopardise British accession.[28] A major SPD objection to the Franco-German Friendship Treaty was the fear that it might exclude Britain, and Wehner therefore suggested an analgous treaty with Britain.[29] SPD statements in favour of British entry were made at regular intervals throughout the sixties, culminating in Brandt's statements to the Hague and Paris Summits. They were habitually couched in terms of the necessity for an accommodation between the EEC and EFTA, since the SPD was not only interested in as much Scandinavian participation as possible, but was also enthusiastic about a solution for Austria because of its close relations with the SPÖ. While the desire for Scandinavian participation was an old one, the grounds for this had altered from Schumacher's day. For Schumacher Scandinavian entry was desirable because it would mean that there would be a greater chance that the European institutions would operate in a socialist direction. In the changed SPD policy of Willy Brandt the emphasis had completely shifted, and Scandinavian entry was valued because of the support it would provide for 'Ostpolitik'.

> The first reason is our common interest in a permanent and viable European Peace Order. That is the **primary** goal of present day West German foreign policy and here we are in agreement with the Scandinavians — the good relations of the Nordic States with Eastern Europe should help in accomplishing important preparatory tasks in the work of European co-operation. I should like to thank our Scandinavian friends for defending the Federal government both officially and unofficially against many unjustified attacks. This has really helped the new government. We are well aware of how important the support of other states, particularly the Scandinavian ones, will be to us in the future.[30]

As a one time Norwegian citizen, Willy Brandt did not confine his efforts for Scandinavian participation solely to West Germany, and he played an active part in the Norwegian Referendum campaign of Autumn 1971.

The SPD has, also because of the awareness of its leaders of the dimensions of Germany's guilt and its close relations with the ruling political elite in Israel, been a consistent and outspoken supporter of close relations between Israel and the Common Market.[31].

Attitudes to Spain and Greece

So far I have considered the efforts of the SPD on behalf of states with which it wished the EEC to have a better relationship. An insight into the party's position can also be gained by examining its views on the relations to be adopted by the EEC towards the European dictatorships.

The SPD maintained an attitude of outright hostility to the Franco regime and support for the exiled Republicans throughout the fifties and early sixties. A suggestion by Serres, the CDU Chairman of the External Trade Committee of the Bundestag, that Spain ought to be a member, or at least an associate member, of the EEC produced a furious attack from SPD Deputy Seifriz.[32] However, by 1965, when the chances of coming to power appeared much brighter, the SPD Executive Committee began to revise its attitude towards Spain and Erler accepted an invitation to visit it.[33] Significantly, the invitation was extended to Erler and not to Brandt, who in the Spanish Government's view was too identified with Republican forces because of his activities during the Spanish Civil War. Since that period the SPD, while not pressing for a Spanish association with the EEC, has not opposed the accommodation between the EEC and Spain.

While the SPD revised its attitude towards Spain, it took the lead in asking for measures against the military dictatorship in Greece. The SPD was particularly responsive to the situation there because of the large number of Greek 'Gastarbeiter' (guest workers) who are members of German trade unions. The SPD Parliamentary Party therefore introduced a resolution asking for Greece's expulsion from the Council of Europe and the suspension of the Association Agreement.[34] Under this pressure from his party, and aware of the strong feelings in the Scandinavian countries, Brandt took what had become for him an uncharacteristically strong line in relation to Greece.[35]

'Ostpolitik' and European integration

In the early years of the Federal Republic, the SPD had consistently maintained that 'Westpolitik' and 'Ostpolitik' were interconnected, and that Adenauer's single-minded pursuit of 'Westpolitik' was excluding any real chance of progress on 'Ostpolitik'. After the failure of the Deutschland plan in 1959, the SPD concentrated, as we have seen, on 'Westpolitik' and indeed laid more emphasis on the need for Western solidarity than the governing coalition. This apparent complete acceptance of the Adenauer foreign policy postulates of the fifties was to a certain extent deceptive. Erler and Wehner and the Parliamentary Party, confronted with the obvious lack of public sympathy for their proposals, had logically enough decided to make changes in the foreign policy of the party analogous to those that had been carried out in the domestic policy of the party at Bad Godesberg in 1959. After the Federal Election of 1961 was over, Willy Brandt on the other hand was moved less by electoral and party considerations than by the weaknesses in the policy positions of both the government and the SPD revealed by the Berlin crisis. Brandt was helped in his reconsideration of accepted policy positions by his constant contact with Egon Bahr, then Press Speaker of the Berlin Senate and undoubtedly the most important influence on Brandt throughout the sixties. It was Bahr, in a speech on 15 July 1963 at the Protestant Academy in Tutzing, who made clear the lines along which Brandt's rethinking of West German foreign policy were running. The basic thrust of this speech is an attempt to apply the principles of John F. Kennedy's 'The Strategy of Peace' to the problem of German unity in the 'post-Wall era'. Bahr called for an end to the policy confrontation, of 'all or nothing' with respect to the German question. Rather than working to overthrow the GDR, attempts ought to be made to change it. This would only be possible through a policy of rapprochement. This policy of 'Wandel durch Annäherung' (change through rapprochement) was to be extraordinarily influential and really provided the leading motive in SPD thinking in the years to come. Such a policy towards the East, unlike the old one of confrontation, was likely to have a marked effect on 'Westpolitik'. It implied a de-emphasising of the single-minded pursuit of Western unification and an emphasis on solutions that would include the whole of Europe. Given West German hostility towards the East in the aftermath of the Wall, these were unpalatable things for a leading politician to say publicly (this was why Bahr, and not Brandt, had made the first public declaration as a *ballon d'essai*) and in an oblique manner, Brandt signalled the way his thinking was developing in his speech in favour of de Gaulle in May 1964.[36]

By the time of the formation of the Grand Coalition in 1966, hostility towards the East among the public at large had abated and Brandt had begun to formulate his ideas more clearly. Brandt, preoccupied with the problems of peace and the German question, sought an answer in a 'European Peace Order': 'We need an orientation which places the German question in their European context and for this we need a concept which contains the bases of a European Peace Order.'[37]

This European Peace Order would only be maintained if there were a European security system. In Brandt's view, a European security system could exist on the basis of a relationship between NATO and the Warsaw Pact, or it could be achieved by the gradual dismantling of these alliances and their replacement by a different system.[38] In the period of the Grand Coalition Brandt seemed to favour the first model, but since 1970 he has often seemed closer to the second view. His final position is obviously dependent on the position taken by the United States government, and only a fairly massive withdrawal from Europe would result in a definitive West German commitment to the second type of European security system.

In the framework of the European Peace Order the EEC plays an important, but secondary, role.

> We are surely in agreement that our community should not be a new block but an exemplary system, which should serve as an important part of a balanced European Peace system. It is in this sense that the Federal Republic of Germany seeks understanding with the East with the co-operation and agreement of her Western partners.[39]

Brandt's thought about the future shape of Europe, which revolves around the problems of 'peace' and East—West relations is thus almost bound to be hostile to the development of a strongly supranational EEC. Aware of the strong emotional identification with 'Europe' both within the SPD and in the West German population at large, Brandt is unlikely ever to attack the idea of a supranational Europe in an unambiguous manner.

In an interview with Gunter Gaus, Egon Bahr was much more outspoken on the tension between a supranational Western Europe and 'Ostpolitik' than Willy Brandt ever has been, but there is little reason to doubt that similar considerations have weighed heavily with Brandt though they will only continue to be influential if the prospects are hopeful for 'Ostpolitik'.

> *Gaus*: Let us assume that you would have the choice between the Europe of the national fatherlands and the Europe which has left the national units behind. Let us assume this: from the standpoint of sentimental value which, you said, every high-quality political man needs ... do you decide in favour of the national solution?
>
> *Bahr*: Yes, of course, because it [the national solution] embraces within it the *tremendous progress toward Eastern Europe and toward the East European peoples,* whereas to the contrary I fear — that may not be right, but I fear — that the other [the political unification of Western Europe] can be obtained *only at the price of renunciation* [of 'Ostpolitik'].
>
> *Gaus*: You mean that Eastern Europe will not be able to come along on the other road?
>
> *Bahr*: Yes!

Gaus: Does that mean a slowing down in the realisation of the West European ideas which were developed in the 1950s?
Bahr: The ideas of the 1950s no longer exist in that form in practical policy. Because that which we do today is an *especially qualified form of co-operation with the aim of a political union, but no longer of supranationality* ...[40]

Conclusion

This survey of SPD attitudes to the Brussels institutions has revealed almost as great changes in the party's attitudes as in the early fifties. Yet these changes have received suprisingly little attention. This lack of attention can be explained in various ways. The first obvious factor is that once the question of entry into the Common Market had been settled the 'European question' lost much of its dramatic quality and became fragmented into a number of issues. While some of these issues, like the question of the proper West German response to Gaullism, were of great importance, they neither gave rise to great internal controversy in the SPD, nor did they tend to polarise out the SPD and the CDU. It was rather a case of the SPD, FDP and most of the CDU combining to defeat the CSU and the rump of the CDU. Perhaps most important, however, has been the dominance in the discussion of West German foreign policy options of 'Ostpolitik'. This dominance is I think easy to understand. 'Ostpolitik' had been virtually neglected throughout the Adenauer period.

More fundamentally, 'Ostpolitik' involves intra-German policy and relations with the GDR. This in turn has required that West Germany decide whether the Federal Republic or some future united Germany should be the basis of her foreign policy. In the fifties these questions had not been raised directly with the GDR, but had played, as we have seen, a very important role in the debate over West German entry into the European institutions. In the late sixties and early seventies they were tackled directly in a number of important treaties concluded by the West German government. These treaties have the effect of playing down the reunification option and emphasising the permanence of the Federal Republic. Such a situation is bound to have repercussions on West European policy. Any present day West German government is going to be less happy about submerging its new found identity and immense prosperity in a tight-knit European construction than the government of the weak and provisional Federal Republic of 1949.

These changes on the part of the SPD have a more than local German

152

importance and contain some important lessons for the British Labour Party. The first is that a deep concern with democracy is quite compatible with Community membership. Secondly, the SPD, even when it was opposed to membership, very quickly gave up focussing its opposition to the European institutions on the issue of loss of sovereignty, since such an attitude tends to look theological and unreal given the realities of today. Thirdly the Labour Party leadership ought to be aware that resistance to a federal Europe is not now confined to Gaullist France, but is also true of the SPD, and that when Brandt talks of 'political and economic union' he has in mind something much less constraining than they imagine. Lastly, acceptance of the EEC has not meant that the SPD has confined its energies to Western Europe. Indeed, the reverse is the case: having initially accepted the principle, the SPD has increasingly concentrated its energies on larger foreign policy questions than those of the relations between Western European states.

Notes

[1]   Wolfram Hanrieder, *The Stable Crisis — Two Decades of German Foreign Policy*, London 1970, p. 158.

[2]   See Waldemar Besson, *Die Aussenpolitik der Bundesrepublik — Erfahrungen und Masstäbe*, Munich 1970, pp. 246–8.

[3]   'SPD gegen Ubertragung des Gaullismus auf Europe' *Stuttgarter Zeitung*, 16 August 1960.

[4]   *Neue Zürcher Zeitung*, 27 January 1963.

[5]   *Stuttgarter Zeitung*, 4 February 1963.

[6]   Ibid.

[7]   *Die Welt*, 21 February 1963.

[8]   *Tatsachen und Argumente*, Sonderausgabe, 3 March 1963, pp. 1–2.

[9]   *Neue Zurcher Zeitung*, 7 March 1963. *Deutsche Zeitung*, 11 and 18 March 1963.

[10]   See W. Besson, op. cit., pp. 312–3.

[11]   Deutscher Bundestag, *Verhandlungen*, 25 April 1963, pp. 3424–32 (H. Wehner); 16 May 1963, pp. 3746–8 (H. Wehner).

[12]   'SPD gibt sich pro-Amerikanisch, Erler bedauert die Absage De Gaulles an England', *Deutsche Zeitung*, 17 January 1963; 'Scharfe Kritik Erlers an der Französichen Politik', *Neue Zürcher Zeitung*, 22 February 1964; 'Erler kritisiert französische Alleingänge', *Stuttgarter Zeitung*, 14 April 1964; 'Gegen "Sonderbündelei" mit Frankreich', *Die Welt*, 12 October 1964.

[13]   *Die Welt,* 16 May 1964; *Stuttgarter Zeitung,* 16 May 1964.

[14]   See G. Ziebura, *Die deutsch–französichen Beziehungen seit 1945 – Mythen und Realitäten,* Pfullingen 1970, p. 134.

[15]   See for example '7-Punkte Programm Willy Brandts', *Neue Zürcher Zeitung,* 11 July 1964.

[16]   Europäisches Parlament, *Verhandlungen,* Ausführliche Sitzungs Berichte NRT8 1965–66, pp. 113–22.

[17]   SPD Resolutions, Drucksachen IV/20911, IV/2211, IV/2212, IV/3129; Bundestag Resolution, Drucksache IV/3665.

[18]   Drucksache IV/3130.

[19]   See especially G. Ziebura, op. cit., p. 133.

[20]   Willy Brandt, *Reden und Interviews 1968–69,* Presse und Informationsamt der Budesregierung, Bonn 1969, pp. 76–81.

[21]   *Bundeskanzler Brandt Reden und Interviews,* Hamburg 1971, pp. 47–54.

[22]   *Das Parlament,* 27 January 1973.

[23]   For the details which indicate that there may also have been other reasons which prompted his joining the CDU see: K.P. Schulz, 'Nach dem Sieg im Herbst wücherten die roten Zellen', *Die Welt,* 23 October 1971; 'Politik der Bundesregierung schadet Deutschland und Europa', *Die Welt,* 5 November 1971; 'Europa Fehlentscheidung der SPD', *Rheinischer Merkur,* 5 November 1971.

For some acid comments on the depth of Schulz's European commitment see *Europäische Gemeinschaft* 11/1971, p. 6.

[24]   Wolfram Hanrieder, *West German Foreign Policy 1949–63 – International Pressure and Domestic Response,* Stanford 1967, pp. 218–9.

[25]   *Die Welt,* 22 March 1963.

[26]   *Die Welt,* 12 October 1964.

[27]   *Neue Zürcher Zeitung,* 15 July 1964.

[28]   *News from Germany* XVI, no. 2 (February 1962), pp. 3–4.

[29]   See note 5.

[30]   See 'Skandinavien und Europa' in W. Brandt, *Aussenpolitik Deutschlandpolitik Europapolitik,* Berlin 1968, pp. 74–81.

[31]   For Brandt's speech to EEC Council of Ministers, 10 May 1967, see ibid., p. 53.

[32]   'SPD Attacke gegen Spaniens EWG Beitritt', *Badische Neueste Nachrichten,* 13 March 1962. This attitude persisted until 1964. See the contributions by P. Blachstein and A.M. Renger in the Council of Europe discussions on Spain reprinted in *Tatsachen Argumente* Sonderausgabe XXV November 1964

[33]   'SPD überprüft ihr Verhältnis zu Spanien', *Ruhr Nachrichten,*

15 January 1965; 'SPD entdeckt Spanien', *Frankfurter Neue Presse*, 7 April 1965; 'Spanien und die EWG', *Die Neue Gesellschaft*, vol. 12, no. 2, March/April 1965, pp. 656–7.

34 Drucksache, V/1989.

35 See W. Brandt, op. cit., p. 127.

36 See note 13 above.

37 W. Brandt 'Fur ein geregeltes Nebeneinander', 2 July 1967, in W. Brandt, op. cit., pp. 80–9. Citation, p. 85.

38 Ibid., p. 86.

39 Declaration by Willy Brandt at the EEC Summit Conference in The Hague, 4 December 1969. Reproduced in *Bundeskanzler Brandt — Reden und Interviews*, op. cit., pp. 47–55. Citation, p. 47.

40 Interview on the television programme 'Zu Protokoll' 4 June 1972. Cited Walter F. Hahn, 'West Germany's Ostpolitik. The Grand Design of Egon Bahr' *Orbis* Winter 1973, p. 879.

Bibliography

Party archives

Material from the Party Executive Archive, formerly in the Party Library in Bonn, now in the Archiv der Sozialendemokratie, Bad Godesberg.

A *Nachlass Kurt Schumacher*

  1 Articles 1945–52 (Q.6)
  2 Interviews (Q.7)
  3 Statements to the Press (Q.8)
  4 Speeches 1947, 1948 (Q.9)
  5 Speeches 1949 (Q.10)
  6 Speeches 1950 (Q.11)
  7 Speeches 1951–2 (Q12)
  8 Press conferences (Q.14)
  9 Correspondence (Q.21-7)

B *Nachlass Erich Ollenhauer*

  1 Ollenhauer–Adenauer 1952–61
  2 Rearmament
  3 Speeches and articles 1947–51
  4 Speeches and articles 1952
  5 Speeches and articles 1953
  6 Speeches and articles January–June 1954
  7 Speeches and essays July–December 1954
  8 Speeches 1955
  9 Monnet Committee

C *Nachlass Fritz Erler*

D *General foreign Policy*

  Schuman Plan (Q.17)
  Foreign policy until 1951 (J.33)
  Foreign policy 1951–55 (J.34)
  EDC (J.35)

Debate on rearmament after 1945 (J.37)
European questions after 1945 (J.39)
The Saar question after 1945 (J.40)
The Saar question after 1945 – economic aspects (J.41)
Schuman Plan (J.42)

E *Debate on party programmes* (K7–9)

F *Correspondence of the Party Executive* with the Berlin section of the party (N.2)

G I visited the Berlin, Bremen and Hamburg sections of the Party but found no particularly useful material. In Bremen, however, I was granted access to Wilhelm Kaisen's private archive, some of which is now to be found in the Archiv der Sozialdemokratie.

H *Fraktionsarchiv*

Protokoll der Fraktionssitzungen 1949–52.

Publications of the Party Executive and groups within the party

1 *Protokoll der Verhandlungen des Parteitages der Sozial demokratischen Partei Deutschlands*

(i) Hamburg 1950
(ii) Dortmund 1952
(iii) Berlin 1954
(iv) Munich 1956

2 *Jahrbuch der SPD* issued yearly by Party Executive

3 *Sopade, Querschnitt durch Politik und Wirtschaft, Sozialdemokratische Parteikorrespondenz* issued monthly 1949–55

4 *Europa-Brücke* – organ of the German section of the Socialist Movement for the United States of Europe.

Pamphlets and other publications

'Aktions-Programm der Sozialdemokratischen Partei Deutschlands, Beschlossen auf dem Dortmunder Parteitag am 28. September 1952. Mit einem Vorwort von Dr Kurt Schumacher' SPD Party Executive, Bonn, October 1952 (pamphlet)

'Aktions–Programm der Sozialdemokratischen Partei Deutschlands, Beschlossen auf dem Dortmunder Parteitag am 28. September 1952, Erweitert auf dem Berliner Parteitag am 24. Juli 1954. Mit einem Vorwort von Dr Kurt Schumacher', SPD Party Executive, Bonn, September 1954 (pamphlet)

'Dokumentation. Acht Jahre sozialdemokraticher Kampf um Einheit, Frieden und Freiheit. Ein dokumentarischer Nachweis der gesamtdeutschen Haltung der Sozialdemokratie und ihrer Initiativen', SPD Party Executive, Bonn 1953 (typewritten, duplicated)

'Entschliessung zur Frage des Verteidigungsbeitrages' Party Executive and Party Committee on 20 January 1952, Bonn, N.D.

Erler, Fritz, M.d.B. 'Soll Deutschland rüsten? Die SPD zum Wehrbeitrag' SPD Party Executive, Bonn, September 1952

Ollenhauer, Erich 'Vor Entscheidungen für Jahrzehnte, Die Stellung der SPD zu den politischen Fragen der Gegenwart' SPD Party Executive, Bonn, N.D.

Ollenhauer, E. '1953, das Jahr der Entscheidungen, Referat des Vorstzenden der Sozialdemokratischen Partei Deutschlands Erich Ollenhauer auf dem Wahlkongress der SPD am 10. Mai 1953 in Frankfurt am Main' Bonn, N.D. (pamphlet)

Ollenhauer, E. 'Nach der Entscheidung, Die Rede Erich Ollenhauers vor den leitenden Funktionären der SPD am 17. September 1953 in Bonn', SPD Party Executive, Bonn, September 1953 (pamphlet)

'Zur Parteidiskussion, Empfehlungen des Parteivorstandes und des Parteiausschusses' SPD Party Executive, Deutz, N.D.

'1863/1963: Programme der Deutschen Sozialdemokratie' Bundessekretariat der Jungsozialisten, Bonn; Hanover 1963

'Protokoll vom Sozialdemokratischen Wahlkongress 1953, am Sonntag, dem 10. Mai 1953, 10.30 Uhr, in der Kongresshalle der Stadt Frankfurt am Main' SPD Party Executive, Bonn; Frankfurt, N.D.

Schmid, Carlo, Prof. 'Die Aussenpolitik der SPD' SPD Party Executive Bonn; Hanover, N.D.

Schulz, Klaus-Peter 'Vor der schwersten Entscheidung ... Deutschland und die Verteidigung Europas – der Standpunkt der Sozialdemokratie' SPD Party Executive, Hanover; Dortmund, N.D.

Schumacher, Dr Kurt 'Ein neues Deutschland, ein neues Europa' Berlin, 22 January 1947; Berlin-Wilmersdorf, N.D. (pamphlet)

Schumacher, K. 'Der "Nationalismus" der SPD' SPD Hanover, March 1949 (pamphlet)

Schumacher, K. 'Europa oder Europa-AG?', Hanover 1950

Schumacher, K. 'Die deutsche Sicherheit! Die Sozialdemokratie zur Verteidigung Deutschlands' SPD Party Executive, Hanover 1950

Schumacher, K. 'Deutschlands Beitrag für Frieden und Freiheit, Die Politik der deutschen Sozialdemokratie in der gegenwärtigen Situation, Dr Kurt Schumachers Referat auf der gemeinsamen Tagung der SPD, Körperschaften am 17. September 1950 in Stuttgart' SPD Party Executive, Dortmund

Schumacher, K. 'Deutschlands Forderung: Gleiches Risiko, gleiches Opfer, gleiche Chancen!' SPD Party Executive, Hanover; Dortmund 1950

Schumacher, K. 'Durch freie Wahlen zur Einheit Deutschlands' SPD Party Executive, Hanover; Dortmund, N.D. (pamphlet: Schumacher's speech in the Bundestag on 9 March 1951, together with the Bundestag resolution of the same day and the letter from Schumacher to Adenauer on 31 January 1951)

Schumacher, K. 'Ein Winter der Entscheidungen' SPD Party Executive, Bonn (after an address given on Hesse Radio on 5 October 1951)

Schumacher, K. 'Die Staatsgewalt geht von den Besatzungsmächten aus' SPD Party Executive, Bonn; Mainz, N.D. (pamphlet)

Schumacher, K. 'Macht Europa stark! Referat Dr. Kurt Schumachers in der gemeinsamen Sitzung des Parteivorstandes, des Parteiausschusses, der Kontroll-Kommission und des Vorstandes der Bundestagsfraktion der SPD am Sonnabend, dem 31. März 1951 in Bonn' SPD Party Executive, Hanover; Dortmund, N.D. (pamphlet)

Schumacher, K. 'Das Volk soll entscheiden! Für die deutsche Gleichberechtigung, Rede des Bundestagsabgeordneten Dr Kurt Schumacher am 8. November 1950' SPD Party Executive, Dortmund, N.D. (pamphlet)

Schumacher, K. 'Fünfzig Jahre mit gebundenen Händen' Hanover 1951

Schumacher, Kurt, Ollenhauer, Erich and Schmid, Carlo 'Das Programm der Opposition, Die drei Vorsitzenden der sozialdemokratischen Bundestagsfraktion über die Ziele der Opposition'. Appendix: 'Das Aktionsprogramm der SPD und die Dürkheimer 16 Punkte der SPD' Hanover; Lübeck, November 1949 (pamphlet)

'Sechs Jahre Ringen um Deutschlands Wiedervereinigung' SPD Party Executive, Bonn, July 1955 (Sopade-Informationsdienst, Denkschriften 57)

'Sozialdemokratie und Bundeswehr' SPD Berlin and Hanover 1957

'Sozialdemokratie und Wehrfrage, Dokumente aus einem Jahrhundert Wehrdebatten' Karl Drott, Berlin and Hanover 1956

SPD Party Executive 'Die Europapolitik der Sozialdemokratie' SPD, Bon 1953

SPD Party Executive 'Die fesseln der deutschen Politik: General-Vertrag und EVG-Vertrag. Sozialdemokratische Stellungnahme im Bundestag bei der ersten Lesung der Verträge' SPD, Bonn 1952

SPD Party Executive 'Frankreich und der Schumanplan: Aus der Schumanplan-Debatte des französischen Parlaments vom 6. und 7. Dezember 1951' SPD, Bonn 1951

SPD Party Executive 'Für ein freies Deutschland in einem neuen Europa' SPD, Hanover 1949

SPD Party Executive 'Für eine Gemeinschaft von Freien und Gleichen! Erich Ollenhauers Rede vor dem Plenum des Bundestages in der 2. Lesung über den Generalvertrag und das EVG-Abkommen' SPD, Bonn 1953

SPD Party Executive 'Generalvertrag. EVG-Abkommen. Ja – dass geht uns alle an!' SPD, Bonn 1953

SPD Party Executive 'Generalvertrag und EVG-Abkommen: Kein Weg zu Europe! Die sozialdemokratische Stellungnahme bei der zweiten Lesung der Verträge "Generalvertrag" und "EVG-Abkommen" im Bundestag vom 3. bis 5. Dezember 1952' SPD, Bonn 1953

SPD Party Executive 'Götterdämmerung beim Schumanplan' SPD, Bonn 1953

SPD Party Executive 'Kommunique' 16 October 1954

SPD Party Executive 'Das Programm der Opposition: Einheit, Freiheit und Frieden für ganz Deutschland' SPD, Bonn 1954

SPD Party Executive 'Der Schumanplan führt nicht nach Europa! Eine Zusammenstellung der wichtigsten Argumente der sozialdemokratischen Redner der grossen Schumanplandebatte vom 9. Januar bis 11. Januar 1952 im Bundestag' SPD, Bonn 1952

SPD Party Executive 'Schwere Niederlage des Bundeskanzlers: Der Vorsitzende der Sozialdemokratischen Partei Deitschlands und Oppositionsführer im Bundestag Erich Ollenhauer zur gegenwärtigen Lage nach dem Scheitern der EVG' Bonn, 1954

SPD Party Executive 'The Social Democratic Party of Germany', SPD, Bonn 1954

SPD Party Executive 'Sozialdemokratie und Wehrbeitrag', (parts I and II), SPD, Bonn 1952

SPD Party Executive 'Trotz Ratifizierung: Der Kampf um die Einheit geht weiter' SPD, Bonn 1955

SPD Party Executive 'Verträge – Deutschlands Schicksal' SPD, Bonn 1954

SPD Party Executive 'Was weisst Du vom Schumanplan?' SPD, Bonn 1951

SPD Party Executive 'Wer Deutschland opfert, opfert Europa' SPD, Bonn 1951

SPD Party Executive 'Wesen und Werden der Sozialistischen Internationale' SPD, Bonn 1952

SPD Party Executive 'Ziele und Aufgaben des Demokratischen Sozialismus: Erklärung der Sozialistischen Internationale, beschlossen in Frankfurt a. Main am 3. Juli 1951' SPD, Bonn 1951

SPD pamphlet not issued with Executive approval

Knothe, Willy Jr., *Der Weg der Sozialdemokratie zur Völkerverständigung und zur friedlichen Vereinigung Deutschlands* — Frankfurt, December 1951

Publications by German socialists in exile

Eichler, W., *Towards European Unity — Franco-German Relations,* London 1942

Fliess, W., *The Economic Reconstruction of Europe*, ISK, London 1943

Die sozialistische Republik — Programm des ISK, London 1939

Luetkens, G., 'A New Order for Germany' Peace Aims Pamphlet, Oxford 1941

Neu Beginnen, Was es will, was es ist und wie es würde, Auslandsbüro, London 1939

Neu Beginnen, *Der Kommende Weltkrieg, Aufgaben und Ziele des deutschen Sozialismus*, Selbstverlag des Verfassers, Paris 1939

Ritzel, Hans, and Bauer, H., *Von der eidgenössischen zur europäischen Föderation* Europa Verlag, Zurich 1940

Ritzel, Hans, and Bauer, H., *Kampf um Europa von der Schweiz aus gesehen*, Europa Verlag, Zurich 1945

Ritzel, Hans, *Europa und Deutschland, Deutschland und Europa*, Karl Drott, Offenbach/Main 1947

Socialist Vanguard Group, *Calling all Europe*, London 1942

Uhlmann, Arno, *Vorstellungen über die Sozialdemokratie in Deutschland nach dem Sturz der Hitler Diktatur*, Londoner Vertretung der SPD, 1943

Vogel, Hans, *Germany and the Post War World*, SPD, London 1944

Walter, Paul, *Sozialistische Revolution gegen Nazi — Imperialismus Zur Politik der SAP*, SAP Ortsgruppe, London 1943

Books by participants, particularly SPD politicians

Adenauer, Konrad, *Erinnerungen* vols. 1-4, 1945–53, '53–55, '55–59, '59–63, DVA, Stuttgart 1965–69. Vol. 1 has been published in English as *Memoirs 1945–53*, Weidenfeld and Nicolson, London 1966

Brandt, Willy, and Löwenthal, Richard, *Ernst Reuter – Ein Leben für Freiheit*, Kindler Verlag, Berlin 1957

Brandt, W., *Aussenpolitik, Deutschlandpolitik, Europapolitik*, Berlin Verlag, Berlin 1968

Brandt, W., *Reden und Interviews 1968–9*, Presse und Informationsamt der Bundesregierung, Bonn 1969

Brandt, W., *A Peace Policy for Europe*, Weidenfeld and Nicolson, London 1969

Brandt, W., *Bundeskanzler Brandt – Reden und Interviews*, Hoffman und Campe, Hamburg 1971.

Brauer, Max, *Nüchternen Sinnes und Heissen Herzens*, Verlag Auerdruck, Hamburg 1953

Erler, Fritz, *Democracy in Germany*, Harvard UP, 1965

Erler, Fritz, *Politik für Deutschland*, Seewald Verlag, Stuttgart 1968

Fimmen, Edo, *Labour's Alternative. The United States of Europe or Europe Ltd.*, The Labour Publishing Co., London 1924

Geyer, Curt, *Gollancz in German Wonderland*, Hutchison, London 1942

Heine, Fritz, *Dr Kurt Schumacher – ein demokratischer Sozialist – europäischer Prägung*, Musterschmidt, Göttingen 1969

Hirschfeld, H., and Reichardt, H., *Ernst Reuter; Aus Reden Und Schriften*, Colloqium Verlag, Berlin 1963

Hoegner, Wilhelm, *Der schwierige Aussenseiter – Erinnerungen eines Abgeordneten, Emigranten und Ministerpräsidenten*, Isar Verlag, Munich 1959

Kaisen, Wilhelm, *Meine Arbeit, Mein Leben*, List Verlag, Munich 1967

Kreyssig, Dr G., *Wirtschaftliche Organisation oder Untergang Europas*, Verlag K. Drott, Offenbach/Main 1947

Löbe, Paul, *Der Weg war Lang*, Arani Verlag, Berlin 1954

Moch, Jules, *Le Réarmament allemand depuis 1950*, Laffont, Paris 1965

Olichewski, Walther, and Scholz, A., *Turmwächter der Demokratie*, a three volume edition of Schumacher's speeches, Arani, Berlin 1954

Schmid, Carlo, *Deutschland und der europäische Rat, Schriftenreihe des Deutschen Rates der Europäischen Bewegung*, 1949

Schmid, Carlo, *Der Weg des deutschen Volkes nach 1945*, SFB Verlag, Berlin 1967

Schmidt, Helmut, *Strategie des Gleichgewichts — Deutsche Friedenspolitik und die Weltmächte*, Ullstein, Berlin 1970

Schumacher, Kurt, *Nach dem Zusammenbruch — Gedanken über Demokratie und Sozialismus*, Karl Strutz, Hamburg 1946

Schulz, K.P., *Sorge um die deutsche Linke — eine kritische Analyse der SPD Politik seit 1945*, Verlag Wissenschaft und Politik, Cologne 1954

Schulz, K.P., *Opposition als politisches Schicksal*, Verlag Wissenschaft und Politik, Cologne 1959

Wesemann, Fried., *Ein Leben für Deutschland*, Herkulverlag, Frankfurt/ Main 1952

General non-SPD

Alleman, Fritz Rene, *Bonn ist nicht Weimar*, Kiepenheuer und Witsch, Cologne/Berlin 1956,

Ashkenasi, Abraham, *Reformpartei und Aussenpolitik: Die Aussenpolitik der SPD, Berlin-Bonn*, Westdeutscher Verlag, Cologne 1968

Baring, Arnulf, *Aussenpolitik in Adenauer's Kanzlerdemokratie; Bonns Beitrag zur europäischen Verteidigungsgemeinschaft Munich*, Oldenburg 1969

Besson, Waldemar, *Die Aussenpolitik der Bundesrepublik — Erfahrungen und Masstäbe*, Piper Verlag, Munich 1970

Bölling, Klaus, *Republic in Suspense — Politics, Parties and Personalities in Post War Germany*, Pall Mall, London 1964

Bung, Hubertus, 'Die Auffassungen der verschiedenen sozialistischen Parteien von den Problemen Europas' Diss., Saarbrücken 1956

Chalmers, David, *The Social Democratic Party of Germany From Working Class Movement to Modern Political Party*, Yale UP, New Haven and London 1964

Coudenhove Kalergi, Richard N., *Pan Europa*, Pan Europa Verlag, Leipzig 1926

Dallin, David, *Soviet Foreign Policy after Stalin,* Methuen, London 1960

Deutsch, Karl, and Edinger, Lewis J., *Germany Rejoins the Powers, Mass Opinion, Interest Groups and Elites in Contemporary German Foreign Policy*, Stanford University Press, Stanford 1959

Dormann, Manfred, *Demokratische Militärpolitik — Die Allierte Militärstrategie als Thema deutscher Politik 1949—68*, Verlag Rombach, Freiburg 1970

Edinger, Lewis, *Kurt Schumacher, A Study in Personality and Political Behaviour*, Oxford University Press, London 1965

Erdmann, K.D., *Adenauer in der Rheinlandpolitik nach dem ersten Welt-krieg*, Klett Verlag, Stuttgart 1966

Flechtheim, Ossip, *Dokumente zur parteipolitischen Entwicklung in Deutschland*, vols. 1–9, Benten Dokumenten Verlag, 1966 ff.

Frankel, Joseph, *National Interest*, Macmillan, London 1970

Freymond, Jacques, *The Saar Conflict 1945–55*, Stevens, London 1960

Friedrich, *Opposition ohne Alternative, Über die Lage der parlamentarischen Opposition im Wohlsfahrstaat*, Verlag Wissenschaft und Politik, Cologne 1962

Gaus, Günter, *Staatserhaltendede Opposition oder hat die SPD kapituliert? Gespräche mit Herbert Wehner*, Roro Aktuell, Reinbek bei Hamburg 1966

Grosser, A., *La Démocratie de Bonn*, Editions Seuil, Paris 1958

Haas, Ernst, *The Uniting of Europe: Political Social and Economic Forces 1950–57*, Stanford University Press, Stanford 1958

Hallstein, Walter, and Baade, F., *Probleme des Schuman Plans*, Kieler Vorträge, Kiel 1951

Hanrieder, Wolfram, *West German Foreign Policy 1949–63 – International Pressure and Domestic Response*, Stanford University Press, Stanford 1967

Hanrieder, Wolfram, *The Stable Crisis – Two Decades of German Foreign Policy*, Harper and Row, London 1970

Heidenheimer, Arnold J., *Adenauer and the CDU. The Rise of the Leader and the Integration of the Party*, Nijhoff, The Hague 1960

Hirsch-Weber, Wolfgang, and Schütz, Klaus, *Wähler und Gewählte, Eine Untersuchung der Bundestagswahlen 1953*, Schriften des Instituts für Politische Wissenschaft Berlin 1957

Hrbek, R., *Die SPD Deutschland und Europe. Die Haltung der Sozialdemokratie zum Verhältnis von Deutschlandpolitik und West Integration 1945–57*, Europa-Union Verlag, Bonn 1973

Kirchheimer, Otto, *Politics Law and Social Change*, (ed. Burin, S., and Shell, K.,) Columbia University Press, New York 1969

Koch, Dieter, *Heineman und die Deutschland Frage*, Chr.Kaiser Verlag, Munich 1972

Kralewski, W., and Neunreither, K.H., *Oppositionelles Verhalten im Ersten Deutschen Bundestag 1949–53*, Westdeutscher Verlag, Cologne-Opladen 1963

Kaden, Albrecht, *Einheit oder Freiheit. Die Weidergründung der SPD 1945/6*, Dietz Verlag, Hanover 1964

Löwke, Udo, *Für den Fall dass: SPD und Wehrfrage 1949–55*, Verlag für Literature und Zeitgeschehen, Hanover 1969

Mahant, Edelgard, 'French and German Attitudes to the Common Market Negotiations' Ph.D., London 1969

Matthias, Erich, *Sozialdemokratie und Nation, Ein Beitrag zur Ideengeschichte der sozialdemokratischen Emigration in der Prager Zeit des Parteivorstandes 1933–38*, D.V.A., Stuttgart 1952

Narr, Wolf Dieter, *CDU-SPD Programm und Praxis seit 1945*, Kohlhammer, Stuttgart 1966

Neubert, Wolfram, *Europäische Integration – Contra Nation und Völkerständigung. Die gegenwärtige Europapolitik und Ideologie der SPD Führung und Ihre Alternative*, Dietz Verlag, Berlin 1964 (Ost)

Neumann, S., 'The New Crisis Strata in German Society', In Morgenthau, H.J. (ed.) *Germany and the Future of Europe*, Chicago University Press, Chicago 1951

Oudenhove, Guy van, *The Political Parties in the European Parliament*, Sijthoff, Leiden 1965

Paterson, W., 'The SPD and European Integration 1949–57 – a Study of "Opposition" in Foreign Affairs', Ph.D. London 1973

Paterson, W., and Campbell, I., *Social Democracy in Post-War Europe*, Macmillan, London 1974

Pirker, Theo, *Die SPD nach Hitler, Die Geschichte der Sozialdemokratischen Partei Deutschlands 1945–64*, Rutten und Loening Verlag, Munich 1965

Ritter, Waldemar, *Kurt Schumacher, Eine Untersuchung seiner politischen Konzeption und seiner Gesellschafts und Staatsauffassung*, Dietz Verlag, Hanover 1964

Rupp, Hans Karl, *Aussenparlamentarische Opposition in der Ära Adenauer – Der Kampf gegen die Atombewaffnung in den fünfziger Jahre*, Paul Rügenstein Verlag, Cologne 1970

Röder, Werner, *Die deutschen sozialistischen Exilgruppen in Gross-Britannien 1940–5*, Verlag für Literature und Zeitgeschehen, Hanover 1969

Schellenger, H.K., *The SPD in the Bonn Republic. A Socialist Party Modernizes*, Martinus Nijhof, The Hague 1968

Schertzinger, Monique, *Conceptions et Positions Européennes du Parti Social Democrate d'Allemagne 1949–54*, Strasbourg 1967

Schmidt, Robert H., *Saar Politik 1945–57*, 3 vols., Düncker und Humboldt, Berlin 1959

Schütz, Klaus, 'Die Sozialdemokratie in Nachkriegsdeutschland' in *Parteien in der Bundesrepublik, Studien zur Entwicklung der deutschen Partei bis zur Bundestags wahl 1953*, Schriften des Instituts für Politische Wissenschaft, Stuttgart 1955

Schwarz, Hans Peter, *Vom Reich zur Bundesrepublik; Deutschland in*

Widerstreit der aussenpolitischen Konzeptionen in den Jahren der Besatzungsherrschaft 1945 bis 1949, Luchterhand, Berlin 1966

Shears, Ursula, 'The Social Democratic Party of Germany, Friend or Foe of European Unity', Diss., Fletcher School of Law and Diplomacy 1959

Speier, Hans, *German Rearmament and Atomic War, The Views of German Military and Political Leaders*, The Rand Corporation, Evanston 1957

Speier, Hans, and Davidson, N.P., *West German Leadership and Foreign Policy*, The Rand Corporation, Evanston 1957

Uhlig, Werner A., *Hat die SPD noch eine Chance?*, Isar Verlag, Munich 1956

Wettig, Gerhard, *Entmilitarisierung und Wiederbewaffnung in Deutschland 1943–45. Internationale Auseinandersetzungen um die Politik der Deutschen in Europa*, Oldenbourg Verlag, Munich 1967

Wildenmann, R., *Partei und Fraktion – ein Beitrag zur Analyse der politischen Willensbildung und des Parteiensystems in der Bundesrepublik*, Verlag Anton Hain, Meisenheim am Glan 1954

Willes, F. Roy, *France, Germany and the New Europe 1945–63*, Stanford University Press, Stanford 1965

Windsor, P., *City on Leave – A History of Berlin 1945–62*, Chatto and Windus, London 1962

Ziebura, Gilbert, *Die Deutsch-Französichen Beziehungen seit 1945 – Mythen und Realitäten*, Noske Verlag, Pfullingen 1970

Articles by participants

Baade, Fritz 'Wie kann Deutschland verteidigt werden? *Aussenpolitik* vol. 2, no. 4, July 1951, pp. 254–62

Baade, Fritz 'Entscheidungen zwischen drei Deutschlandkonzeptionen' *Aussenpolitik* vol. 3, no. 9, September 1952, pp. 558–68

Baade, Fritz 'Nur noch zwei Deutschlandkonzeptionen' *Aussenpolitik* vol. 5, no. 12, December 1954, pp. 153–64

Eichler, Willy 'Verteidigungsbeitrag für die Freiheit' *Geist und Tat*, vol. 7, no. 3, March 1952, pp. 65–73

Erler, Fritz 'Deutschland zwischen den Weltmächten' *Geist und Tat*, vol. 9, no. 2, February 1954, pp. 36–41

Erler, Fritz 'An der Schwelle des Atomzeitalters' *Die Neue Gesellschaft*, vol. 2, no. 1, 1955, pp. 3–9

Erler, Fritz 'The Struggle for German Reunification' *Foreign Affairs*, vol. 34, no. 3, April 1956, pp. 380–94

Gleissberg, Gerhard 'Die Aussenpolitik der deutschen Sozialdemokraten' *Die Zukunft*, September 1952, pp. 251–6

Luetkens, Gerhart 'Die parlamentarische Opposition in der Aussenpolitik' *Aussenpolitik*, vol. 2, no. 6, September 1951, pp. 348–407

Luetkens, Gerhart 'Betrachtungen zu einem Deutschland Vertrag' *Aussenpolitik*, vol. 4, no. 3, March 1953, pp. 141–51

Schmid, Carlo 'Germany and Europe' *International Affairs*, vol. 2, no. 3, July 1951, pp. 306–11

Schmid, Carlo 'Die Aussenpolitik der Machtlosen' *Aussenpolitik*, vol. 3, no. 1, January 1952, pp. 11–19

Schmid, Carlo 'Organizing Europe: The German Social Democratic Program' *Foreign Affairs*, vol. 30, no. 4, July 1952, pp. 531–44

Other articles

Braunthal, Gerhard 'West German Trade Unions and Disarmament' *Political Science Quarterly*, vol. 73, no. 1, March 1958, pp. 82-99

Bretton, Henry L. 'The German Social Democratic Party and the International Situation' *American Political Science Review*, vol. XLVII, no. 4, December 1953, pp. 980–96

Hahn, W. 'West Germany's Ostpolitik: The Grand Design of Egon Bahr' *Orbis*, Winter 1972, pp. 859–80

Heidenheimer, A.J. 'Federalism and the Party System' *American Political Science Review*, vol. VII, no. 3, 1958, pp. 809–28

Heidenheimer, A.J. 'Foreign Policy and Party Discipline in the CDU' *Parliamentary Affairs*, vol. 13, no. 1, 1959, pp. 70–84

Kirchheimer, Otto 'The Waining of Opposition in Parliamentary Regimes' *Social Research*, vol. 26, Summer 1957, pp. 127–56

Loewenstein, Karl 'The Bonn Constitution and the European Defence Community Treaties – A Study in Judicial Frustration' *Yale Law Journal,* vol. 64, no. 6, May 1955, pp. 806–39

Meissner, Wilhelm 'Die Aussenpolitik der SPD' *Deutsche Aussenpolitik*, vol. 1, no. 3, 1956, pp. 396–409

Paterson, W.E. 'Foreign Policy and Stability in West Germany' *International Affairs*, vol. 49, July 1973, pp. 913–30

Schertzinger, Monique 'Le SPD et le Nationalisme' *Revue d'Allemagne*, vol. 1, no. 4, pp. 467–84

Vardys, Stanley 'German Post-War Socialism: Nationalism and Kurt Schumacher 1945–52' *Review of Politics*, 27(2) 1965, pp. 220–44

Wahraftig, S.L. 'Der Weg der Sozialdemokraten zum Dortmunder Parteitag' *Frankfurter Hefte*, vol. 7, no. 11, November 1952, pp. 849–59

Author's interviews and correspondence

The author interviewed the following members of the SPD, dates as specified:

Willi Birkelbach	November 1966
Max Brauer	November 1966
Hans-Eberhard Dingels	July 1967
Willi Eichler	August 1967
Fritz Heine	November 1966
Wilhelm Kaisen	November 1966
Waldemar von Knoeringen	September 1969
Anne-Marie Renger	December 1966
Professor Carlo Schmid	July 1967
Arno Scholz	July 1967
Klaus Schütz	October 1972

Interviews were also held with the following non-members:

Richard Mayne	March 1968
Jules Moch	June 1971
Pierre Uri	March 1967
Hans vom Hoff	July 1967

Correspondence was conducted with Helmut Kalbitzer, Willi Eichler and Waldemar von Knoeringen.

Index

Indexer's note: Organisations are indexed under initials. A list of these with their English equivalent in full appears in the glossary which follows the index.

German re-unification, Soviet proposal for, (1952) 83—6
Germany, Four Power occupation of 4—5; *see also* East Germany; West Germany
Gleissberg. Gerhart 103
Götterdammerung beim Schumanplan (SPD, 1953) 64
Grand Coalition (1966—69) 144—6, 150
Grath, Erwin 37
Greece 148—9
Grotewohl, Otto 10
Grumbach, Salamon 59

Haas, Ernst ix, 14n1, 118, 131
Hague Congress for the United States of Europe (1948) 12, 32—3; *see also* United States of Europe, Monnet's Action Committee for
Hague Summit Conference (1969) 146, 148
Halecki, Oscar 3
Hamburg Conference (1950) 33, 38—42, 52
Hamburg demonstration (1955) 106
Hamburg resolution (1951) 58
Hanover, SPD Congress in (1949) 6
Hanrieder, Wolfram 147
Hastings Conference (1950) 37
Heiland 62
Heine, Fritz 11, 20, 24, 32, 59, 133
Heinemann, Gustav 105
Henssler, Fritz 24, 30, 39, 60—2, 65
Herford demonstration (1955) 106
Het Paarool 32—3
Heuss, Theodor 21, 92
Heydorn 39
High Authority 59, 61, 118, 124
Hilferding, Rudolf 9
Hilpert, Werner 20
Hoegner, Wilhelm 12
Hof demonstration (1955) 106
Hue, Otto 1

IAR 6, 14, 19—44, 49, 52, 55; creation of 22—3
Interviews, author's (with dates) 169
ISK 3

Israel 148

Jacobs 117

Kaisen, Wilhelm 12, 20, 31—3, 39—42, 57—8, 78, 94—5, 101, 104, 120—1, 125
Kalbitzer, Helmut 118, 123, 126, 169
Kautsky, Karl Johann 7, 39, 62
Kennedy, President John F. 147, 150
Kingsbury-Smith, Mr (journalist) 37
Kirchheimer, O. 12, 17n44
Kirkpatrick, I. 7
Kloster Wennigsen Conference (1945) 7
Knothe, Willi, Jr 78
Koch, Dr,54
Kohnstamm, Max 124
Korean war, effect of 72—3, 96
KPD 8, 29, 41—2, 64, 78—9
Kreyssig, Gerhard 117—18
Krushchev 120
Kühn, Heinz 102, 105
Kunze, Max 102

Labour Party (British), *see* British Labour Party
Labour's Alternative Europe or Europe Ltd (Fimmen) 2
Länder politicians 6, 12, 13, 20, 39—40, 58, 75, 81, 105
Lasalle, Ferdinand 7
Löbe, Paul 20—1, 39
London Conference (1954) 103—4
Lüdemann, H. 39
Luetkens, Gerhart 37, 42, 54, 59, 63, 78, 90, 93
Luxembourg Compromise (1966) 145

McLoy, John 7, 72, 86
Maier, Reinhold 95
Margulies, Robert 129
Marshall Plan (and Treaty — 1948) 5, 10, 12, 24, 28, 33
Marx, Karl 7
Mattick, Kurt 142
Mayer, René 116
Mellies, W. 117, 133—4
Memoirs (Adenauer) 27, 132

Schumacher, Kurt 7–14, 19–42 *passim*, 51–9, 64, 72–9, 87; death 89–90
Schuman, Robert (and plan) 4, 36–7, 40–1, 49–66 *passim* 76, 78
Seifriz 149
Serres 149
SFIO 9, 26, 59, 73, 117, 127, 143
Socialist International Conference (1948) 25; (1950) 53 (eleven points of approval for the Schuman plan, 53–4); (1951) 58–9
Socialist Movement for the United States of Europe 125; *see also* United States of Europe, Monnet's Action Committee for
Sokolovsky, Marshal 5
Sorge um die deutsche Linke 100
Soviet Union, *see* USSR
Spaak, Paul Henri 122
Spain 148–9
SPD:
  and Constitutional Court 79–82; and EDC 71–107; and EEC 115–36; and Euratom 122–36; and European Integration, (1958–73) 141–53; and Greece 148–9; and Schuman Plan 49–66 (*see also* Schuman, Robert); and Soviet Démarche on re-unification 85–6; and Spain 148–9; and Trade Union Views 57–8 (*see also* Trade Union Views); and UK 147–8; and USA 147–8; and Western European Union 71–107; attack on Gaullism 141–5; conflicts within (1945–49) 11–14; Congress of Hanover (1949) 6; European manifesto (1964) 145, 147; in London (1940–45) 3–4; opposition to Council of Europe 34–7, 42; opposition to IAR 22–6; opposition to Saar Conventions 36–41; organisation of, machinery of 11
  party meeting venues:
    Bremen, 1947 36; Bad Dürkheim, 1949 20–1; Cologne, 1949 21, 36; Hamburg, 1950 33, 38–42, 52; Dortmund, 1952 90–2; Berlin, 1954, 101–3, 119; Frankfurt, 1955

105–7; Munich, 1956 125; Ravensburg, 1968 145
  policy (1949–57) 129–36, post war, (1945–49) 4–10; seven point memorandum on Schuman plan 56–7
Steffen, Jochen 147
Stierle, Herr 86
Strategy of Peace (Kennedy's) 150
Strobel, Käte 145
Stuttgarter Zeitung 117
Suhr, Otto 20
Süsterhenn, Dr Adolf 24
SVG 3, 15n18

Tariffs 127, 129
Trade Union Views 57–8, 79, 115–16, 123–4
Truman, President Harry S. 25, 71

UK and SPD 147–8; UK refusal to attend conferences on European integration 60, 63, 65, 127
Unification of Germany 87–8, 100, *see also* German re-unification, Soviet proposal for
United States of Europe, Monnet's Action Committee for 115, 123–9; *see also* Monnet, Jean
Uniting Europe (Haas) ix
USA and SPD 147–8
USSR 3, 83–6

Van Naters, Jonkheer Marinus van der Goes 116–17
Van Nes Ziegler, Johannes 120–1, 125
Veit, Dr H. 54
Versailles, Treaty of 61, 66
Vichy France 9
Von Brentano, H. 143
Von Hassel, K.-U. 144
Vom Hoff, Hans 96
Von Knoeringen, Waldemar 20, 42, 169
Von Thadden 64

Warsaw Pact 150
Washington Conference (1953) 99
Wehner, Herbert 39–40, 59, 85–8,

Glossary

BHE	Refugees Party
CDU	Christian Democratic Union
Comisco	The First Post-war International Grouping of Social Democratic Parties
CSU	Christian Social Union
DGB	German Trade Union Federation
DPS	Saar Social Democratic Party
ECSC	European Coal and Steel Community
EDC	European Defence Council
EEC	European Economic Community
EFTA	European Free Trade Area
ERP	European Recovery Programme
FDP	Free Democratic Party
GDP	All German Party (*sometimes* German Party)
GDR	German Democratic Republic
IAR	International Authority of the Ruhr
ISK	International Socialist Combat Group
KPD	Communist Party
MLF	Multilateral Force
MRP	Popular Republican Movement
MSEUE	Socialist Movement for the United States of Europe
NATO	North Atlantic Treaty Organisation
NB	New Beginnings Group
NPD	National Democratic Party
OEEC	Organisation for European Economic Co-operation
SAP	Socialist Workers' Party
SFIO	French Social Democratic Party
SPD	German Social Democratic Party
SVG	Socialist Vanguard Group
UK	United Kingdom
USA	United States of America
USSR	Soviet Russia
WEU	Western European Union